HERITAGE OF SCOTLAND

EXECUTIVE EDITOR Julian Brown

CREATIVE DIRECTOR Keith Martin

EDITOR Tarda Davison-Aitkins

SENIOR DESIGNER Leigh Jones

DESIGN 2wo Design Ltd

PRODUCTION Sarah Scanlon

PICTURE RESEARCH Charlotte Deane

First published in 2000
by Hamlyn,
an imprint of Octopus Publishing Group Limited
2–4 Heron Quays, London E14 4JP

Copyright © Octopus Publishing Group Limited 2000

ISBN 0 600 59834 9

A catalogue record for this book is
available from the British Library

Produced by Toppan
Printed in China

HERITAGE OF SCOTLAND

A CULTURAL HISTORY OF SCOTLAND & ITS PEOPLE

NATHANIEL HARRIS

hamlyn

CONTENTS

INTRODUCTION

NO SINGLE IMAGE WILL DO TO CAPTURE THE ESSENCE OF SCOT-
LAND. THE MOUNTAINS, LOCHS AND GLENS OF THE
HIGHLANDS; KILTED REGIMENTS MARCHING TO THE SKIRL OF
BAGPIPES; BUSTLING, COSMOPOLITAN GLASGOW AND STATELY
EDINBURGH; THE SMALL TOWNS, FERTILE PLAINS AND ROLLING
HILLS OF THE NOT-SO-LOWLANDS; MARY, QUEEN OF SCOTS AND
BONNIE PRINCE CHARLIE; RUINED CASTLES, STATELY HOMES
AND ONCE-GREAT SHIPYARDS; PLOUGHMEN AND DROVERS
AND GREAT ESTATES GIVEN OVER TO THE GROUSE; QUEEN VIC-
TORIA AND JOHN BROWN; STRICT SABBATARIANISM AND
'WHISKY GALORE' ; BURNS NIGHT AND HOGMANAY – THE LIST
COULD BE EXTENDED ALMOST INDEFINITELY.

Each image, or cluster of images, is true, although only part of the truth. It would
be hard to find a country of comparable size that has such a vital presence, founded on
a rich and turbulent history and set in landscapes of wonderful natural beauty and
human memories. And then there are the Scots themselves. Scottishness takes
many forms, but all of them have proved to be aspects of an enduring national
identity. Out of the clashing and blending of Picts, Romans, Irish, 'ancient'
Britons, Anglo-Saxons, Norwegians, Normans and Flemings, the Scots took their
place in history as a people quite distinct from their English neighbours and more
than willing to meet them on the battlefield.

Over the centuries they zealously defended their independence while quar-
relling violently among themselves; the internal history of the country is full of
coups and civil wars as well as stern struggles based on principle or religion. A
characteristic combination of stubbornness and panache led to glory at Bannockburn and disaster at Flodden, but neither diplomacy nor 'rough wooing'
persuaded the Scots to submit to England. In fact, the first successful Anglo-Scottish accommodation occurred through a dynastic accident which brought a Scots
king to the English throne, although the sequel was hardly a Scottish triumph.

A full union between the two countries took place in 1707, but the Scots
retained national institutions such as their legal and educational systems – and
their stubborn Scottishness. Tens of thousands went on to serve Britain and the
Empire as soldiers, administrators, politicians, scientists, engineers, explorers and
missionaries; in this sense their Britishness was not in doubt, but nothing came of
predictions that their native character would gradually disappear.

This remained true in the late 20th century, when mass media and 'Coca-Cola
culture' were said to be irresistibly forging a uniform, international consumer society. Yet, despite all the pressures, the Scots vernacular and the Gaelic tongue of the
Highlands have survived, Scottish folk music lives on and influences the pop
scene, and the affiliations of modern writers such as Liz Lochhead, Alasdair Gray
and Irvine Welsh are as unmistakable as those of Sir Walter Scott and Robert
Louis Stevenson. The point was emphasized when, as the second millennium
came to an end, Scots once more acquired their own parliament and direct control over their own affairs. The heritage of Scotland can be seen in terms of lovely
landscapes and romantic remains, but it is also a living heritage, linked with the
past through the still vital, obstinate and creative people of Scotland.

THE LAND

ABOVE: Staffa, Fingal's Cave (1812) by J.M.W. Turner on the left and Linlithgow Palace and Loch on the right

Loch Carron and the Skye mountains

ALIVE WITH HISTORY AND A MAGICAL
BEAUTY, THE SCOTTISH LANDSCAPE IS
LIKE NO OTHER. LAKES, MOORS AND
MOUNTAINS, RARE WILDLIFE SPECIES,
BUSTLING CITIES AND QUIET TOWNS,
CASTLES AND ABBEYS, PROVIDE AN
UNEQUALLED VARIETY OF PLEASURES.

VARIETIES OF LANDSCAPE

SCOTLAND IS RENOWNED FOR THE BEAUTY OF ITS HEATHER-COVERED MOORS AND SNOWY MOUNTAINS, STEEP-SIDED GLENS, RUSHING WATERS AND SHIMMERING LOCHS. MOST OF THESE FEATURES ARE ASSOCIATED WITH THE HIGHLANDS, WHICH ARE OFTEN FELT TO BE THE 'REAL' SCOTLAND, OR AT ANY RATE THE SCOTLAND THAT IS MOST WORTH SEEING FOR ITS SCENERY, WILDLIFE AND ROMANTIC HISTORY.

But this view fails to do justice to the country's rich diversity of human and natural landscapes, all concentrated in part of a small island on the Atlantic fringe of Europe. Scotland's physical layout is usually described in terms of a three-region breakdown which distinguishes between the Highlands and Islands, the Central Lowlands and the Southern Uplands. Based on geological features that have shaped the landscape even more fundamentally than human activity, this breakdown is useful even though it ignores the existence of significant variations within each region that add to their attraction. The boundaries are fairly sharply drawn. In the north, the Highlands and Islands are demarcated by 'the Highland Line', which runs roughly south-west along the foothills, from just below Stonehaven, on the east coast, to the Clyde estuary in the west. Below the Highland Line, the Central Lowlands stretch as far as another imaginary line, from Dunbar to Ayr, at which the third main region, the Southern Uplands, begins. These extend to the border with England which, though settled by political conflicts as much as by geography, follows a reasonably natural route from the Solway Firth, through the Cheviot Hills, to the River Tweed.

The Southern Uplands are neither as awe-inspiring nor as forbidding as the Highlands. The hills are relatively uniform in character, being rounded and low (with only a few exceptions, between 300 and 600 metres high), so that they are greatly attractive to walkers. The fast-flowing River Tweed and its many tributaries are celebrated for the beauty of their wooded valleys and the abundance of their salmon and trout. This is sheep country, famous for its woollen textiles. But the area is also filled with memories of a turbulent past

GREY MARE'S TAIL, THE HIGHEST FALLS IN THE BORDERS, IS NOW A WELL-KNOWN TOURIST ATTRACTION, USUALLY VISITED FROM MOFFAT. BUT IN THE 17TH CENTURY THIS WILD SOUTH-WEST COUNTRY WAS A PLACE OF REFUGE AND AMBUSHES, WITNESSING BLOODY ENCOUNTERS BETWEEN PRESBYTERIAN COVENANTERS AND THEIR ROYALIST PERSECUTORS.

THE ROLLING LAMMERMUIR HILLS OCCUPY PARTS OF EAST LOTHIAN AND BERWICKSHIRE, EXTENDING AS FAR AS THE EAST COAST. BEAUTIFUL BUT BLEAK IN BAD WEATHER, THIS IS THE SETTING OF SIR WALTER SCOTT'S NOVEL THE BRIDE OF LAMMERMUIR.

when Scots and English battled on both sides of the border and, even when the kings of both countries were at peace, private wars and lawless plundering went on almost constantly. That is why there are so many small, grim castles and tower-houses, and such spectacularly beautiful ruined abbeys at Melrose, Jedburgh, Kelso and Dryburgh; paradoxically, these were sacked and rebuilt many times, but owed their final decay to the 16th-century Reformation rather than fire and the sword. Stately homes were built close to the Tweed in less anarchic times, notably Traquair House and Abbotsford, the creation of Sir Walter Scott – appropriately so since Scott's own writings were responsible for transforming the brutalities of border feuds into the stuff of romance.

This part of southern Scotland offers some extraordinary contrasts – areas of fertile, carefully farmed land, pleasant market towns, fishing villages and stark, wave-pounded coastlines. On the east coast, the hills give way to lowland, providing an easy route for armies to march into or out of Scotland; just to the south, on the English side of the border, lies Flodden Field, where in 1513 an invading Scottish force under James IV suffered the most catastrophic defeat in the nation's history.

Tucked away in the south-west, Dumfries and Galloway have a quite separate character. Still frequently seen as out of the mainstream of Scottish life, the area is one of considerable charm. The climate is mild and there is much fertile farming land, although the terrain becomes rugged in almost Highland fashion on the coastal peninsulas of far-western Galloway. The Irish coast is visible, only 40 kilometres away, from the southernmost point of the Rhins of Galloway, which thrusts its curious hammerhead into the sea. Rare wildlife species draw nature-lovers to the coastal flats of the south-west and the Galloway Forest Park, while long-distance walkers can start a 340-kilometre trek from Portpatrick along the Southern Upland Way to Cockburnspath on the east coast. By contrast, the old seaport of Kirkcudbright has long boasted an artists' colony, attracted by the delightful character of the town, the climate and the superb sea views. Dumfries is entered from England via Gretna Green, long a first stopping-place for run-away English couples who wished to marry in haste. Dumfries, along with Ayr to the north, is Robert Burns country, where the nation's greatest poet has become a major 'heritage' attraction. Quiet enough now, this was once an area where history was made: Whithorn was the first Christian site in Scotland, the liberator-king Robert Bruce was based in Annandale, and Covenanters and Cameronians took up arms here to defend their religious beliefs against the Stuart kings.

THE HEARTLAND

THE MAJORITY OF SCOTS LIVE IN THE CENTRAL LOW-
LANDS, WHICH HAVE LONG BEEN THE POLITICAL AND
ECONOMIC HEART OF THE COUNTRY. FERTILE LAND,
ACCESSIBLE HARBOURS AND LATER, EXPLOITATION OF
COAL AND IRON DEPOSITS, ALL FAVOURED THE DEVEL-
OPMENT OF TRADE, INDUSTRY AND TOWNS.

The capital, Edinburgh, and the largest city, Glasgow, grew up on
the two great firths (estuaries) of Forth and Clyde, which give Scotland
its distinctive nipped-in-waist, across which the invading Romans built
the Antonine Wall, now in most places no more than stretches of earth
banks and ditches. Stirling owed its importance to the lump of volcanic
rock that provided an ideal location for a castle, especially since this was
superbly sited to control the most important routes into and out of the
Highlands. Perth, Scotland's capital until the late Middle Ages, grew
up at the point where the River Tay opens out to become a firth.
Between them, the Tay and the Forth create the peninsula of Fife, a
large plain whose individuality earned it the nickname 'the wee kingdom'; its most famous city, St Andrews, lacks any obvious geographical
advantages but nevertheless played a crucial role in Scottish history as

ST ANDREWS CASTLE, SPECTACULARLY LOCATED
RIGHT ON THE SEASHORE. ST ANDREWS, A SMALL
TOWN ON THE EAST COAST, WAS THE ECCLESIASTICAL
CAPITAL OF SCOTLAND; SOAKED IN HISTORY, ITS
FAMOUS SIGHTS INCLUDE THE RUINOUS CATHEDRAL
AND OTHER MONUMENTS, THE ANCIENT UNIVERSITY,
AND THE FAMOUS ROYAL AND ANCIENT GOLF CLUB.

an ecclesiastical centre and has the curious
twin distinction of being home to the nation's
oldest university and its favourite game, golf.
Across the Tay from Fife lies another plain,
hemmed in by the Highlands, with its principal town, Dundee, on the coast; despite a
turbulent history during the Middle Ages and

the Reformation, followed by a 19th-century boom as a jute manufacturer, Dundee is popularly known for two solid contributions to human happiness, marmalade and cake.

The Central Lowlands are only low by comparison with the Highlands and Uplands to north and south. Ranges of hills – Sidlaws, Ochils, Campsies and Pentlands – thrust up here and there, dividing the region into relatively small plains. Despite the impact of cities and factories, there are many fine natural environments and views, especially along the firths and the coastline; one impressive example is the Bass Rock, a volcanic plug rising from the sea off the east coast, thickly splashed with guano and inhabited by hosts of gannets and other birds. This area, East Lothian, is the continuation of the lowland route from Northumberland into Scotland, and the witnesses of its former strategic importance include two spectacular castle ruins on the coast, Tantallon and Dunbar. Standing squarely at the climax of the coastal Lowland route, Edinburgh offers innumerable urban pleasures, the sight of its Castle Rock (like Stirling's, a volcanic outcrop) and, on its northern outskirts along the Forth, a mixture of natural and human-made spectacles; these last include one of the greatest engineering feats of the 19th century, the Forth Rail Bridge, its four-span construction still grandly impressive.

In the west, Glasgow has outlived several reputations, flattering and otherwise, and is now accepted as a dynamic modern metropolis with a cultural pedigree challenging Edinburgh's. Formerly the heart of a great shipbuilding industry, the Clyde offers some lovely views and, although the area north of the firth is heavily urbanized, the Highlands are not far away. To the south, in Ayrshire, the character of the country is very different, with pleasant farming country inland and sandy resorts – the Glaswegians' playground – on the coast. Though steeped in history, Ayr itself has taken advantage of a mild climate and long beaches to thrive as a resort as well as a heritage centre, standing at the northern end of a 'Burns Trail' extending to the town of Dumfries on the River Esk above the Solway Firth. Much better known than a few years ago, the entire area has benefited from the presence of an international airport, Prestwick, whose very siting is an advertisement for the good, fog-free weather enjoyed by this corner of a famously misty land.

BASS ROCK IS A CELEBRATED LANDMARK RISING OUT OF THE FIRTH OF FORTH NOT FAR FROM NORTH BERWICK. THIS ANCIENT VOLCANIC PLUG IS NOW A HAVEN FOR WILDLIFE, WITH A VERY LARGE COLONY OF GANNETS.

THE HIGHLANDS AND ISLANDS

SCOTLAND'S MUCH-ADMIRED MOUNTAIN COUNTRY IS ALL LOCATED IN THE NORTH AND NORTH-WEST, ABOVE THE HIGHLAND LINE. THE MOUNTAINS ARE NOT HIGH BY THE EXACTING STANDARDS OF GEOGRAPHERS AND MOUNTAINEERS, BUT THEY ARE SPECTACULAR AND LOVELY, THE RESULT OF GREAT SHIFTS AND UPHEAVALS OF THE ROCKS AND VOLCANIC ERUPTIONS.

Pride of place goes to the several hundred peaks, known as Munros, which reach 3,000 feet (914 metres) or more; they are distributed unevenly over the Highlands, but are only found in two islands, Skye and Mull, which were once part of the mainland. The scenic beauty of the Highlands is largely created by the combination of mountains and long, steep-sided valleys, or glens, which are frequently filled with lakes, which Scots call lochs or, when small, lochans. Depending on the terrain and the time of year, moorland, heather or woods add variety to the landscape, which may also harbour types of wildlife – red deer, golden eagles, seals and wild cats – that are relatively rare in other parts of Britain.

The most formidable ranges are not necessarily the most popular with visitors. Modern tourism began in the Highlands of Argyll, the region just north of the Clyde, where the peaks are relatively modest. The poems and novels of Sir Walter Scott drew attention to the Trossachs, Loch Katrine and Loch Lomond, where long vistas of woods, hills and island-dotted waters first delighted tourists such as the poet William Wordsworth before becoming known to the wider world.

GLENCOE IS A PLACE OF AWE-INSPIRING BEAUTY, ADMIRED FOR ITS ROCKY SKYLINE, WHICH ALSO ATTRACTS CLIMBERS. BUT IT HAS NEVER QUITE SHAKEN OFF THE SINISTER REPUTATION IT ACQUIRED AFTER THE MASSACRE OF GLENCOE, ALTHOUGH THE INFAMOUS SLAYING OF MACDONALD FAMILIES BY GOVERNMENT TROOPS TOOK PLACE OVER THREE CENTURIES AGO.

Further north and east the landscape becomes bleaker. Beyond Glencoe, still notorious for the three-hundred-year-old massacre of the MacDonalds, and the wild, waste swampland of Rannoch Moor, the Grampian mountains rear up, high and close-peaked; among them is Ben Nevis, at 4,406 feet (1,343 metres) the highest peak in the British Isles. Further east, the Cairngorms boast the largest single group of tall peaks, four of which fail to match Ben Nevis by only a hundred metres or so. Here the unyielding masses of the mountains, with their great corries (hollows) and their long passes, represent the Highlands at their most overwhelming. But in the foothills, woods and water exercise a softening influence, and the Cairngorms have become a magnet for those who enjoy energetic leisure pursuits such as climbing, walking and skiing, with Aviemore on the

River Spey as the best-known centre. The Cairngorms are also the backdrop for the Highland Games at Braemar, held in the summer and attended by the royal family during their residence at Balmoral.

Any map of Scotland reveals the violence of the natural forces that have shaped its present appearance, biting into the west coast and stranded islands in innumerable places to create strange, ragged outlines. Equally dramatic is the Great Glen, a huge geological fault which bisects the Highlands from Inverness on the Moray Firth to Fort William at the head of Loch Linnhe. Much of its length is occupied by Loch Lochy and Loch Ness (whose much sought-after monster remains perversely elusive), which since the early 19th century have formed part of the great coast-to-coast Caledonian Canal. Beyond the Great Glen, the North-West Highlands are celebrated for high, crowded ranges and coast-piercing sea-lochs. At Glenfinnan, on the stunningly beautiful Loch Shiel, Bonnie Prince Charlie raised his standard to begin the ill-fated Jacobite Rebellion of 1745. Finally, above Loch Carron, the Highlands reach a wild, stark climax, culminating in the wind-battered cliffs of the coast around Cape Wrath.

As well as the Highlands proper, the region above the Highland Line includes the lowlands of the north-east, which are effectively a continuation of the plain below the Tay. They take in granite-built Aberdeen and the shoulder of land below the Moray Firth; fronting the North Sea, their terrain and the dryer, sharper atmosphere make them very different from the Highlands in which their rivers rise. The traditional farming and fishing economy has been supplemented in recent times by tourism and the impact of drilling for oil in the North Sea. Beyond the Moray Firth, the lowlands of Caithness are intensely bleak, culminating in a dramatic coast with extraordinary wind-cut cliffs and rock arches and stacks along the shoreline. Still further north there are spectacular sights in the Orkneys, whose treeless, wind-blasted landscape drove their Neolithic inhabitants to build in stone, giving permanence to some extraordinary prehistoric dwellings. The Orkneys and further-flung Shetlands were settled by Vikings and, belonging to Scandinavian monarchies till the 15th century, still retain some differences in speech and outlook from their fellow-Scots.

The Western Isles – the Hebrides – share this Norse background and the hard, semi-isolated way of life created by geography and limited resources. Even now, although sea and air services bring them into closer touch with mainland Scotland, the Hebrides preserve a certain feeling of remoteness. This is especially true of the long, loch-sprinkled Outer Hebrides fronting the Atlantic, where crofting (smallholding) is still a way of life. There are also crofts on the Inner Hebrides, of which the best-known to outsiders is Skye, with a mountain spine, the Cuillins, whose profiles are like nothing else in Scotland.

WINTER IN THE HIGHLANDS IS HARSH BUT LOVELY. THE PHOTOGRAPH SHOWS A RED DEER STAG, MAGNIFICENTLY ENDOWED WITH THE ANTLERS THAT HE WILL CAST IN SPRING. DEER ARE FOUND ALL OVER SCOTLAND, BUT ARE MOST NUMEROUS IN THE HIGHLANDS AND ISLANDS, WHICH ARE ALSO HOME TO GOLDEN EAGLES, OSPREYS, WILD CATS AND SEALS.

TURBULENT HISTORY

LEFT: The Wallace Monument on Abbey Craig near Stirling

RIGHT: Statue of Robert Bruce at Bannockburn

SIX THOUSAND YEARS AGO NEW STONE AGE SETTLERS WERE ALREADY ESTABLISHED IN THE ORKNEYS. ON ORKNEY ITSELF THE VILLAGE AT SKARA BRAE HAS BECOME FAMOUS, WHILE THE BURIAL CAIRN AT MAES HOWE REPRESENTS AN EVEN MORE REMARKABLE FEAT OF DRY-STONE (MORTAR-LESS) BUILDING. HUGE BLOCKS WERE USED TO CONSTRUCT THE ENTRANCE PASSAGE (ABOVE) AND THE CHAMBERS

THE SCOTS BECAME AWARE OF THEIR NATIONAL IDENTITY AT A REMARKABLY EARLY DATE, INSPIRED BY LEADERS SUCH AS WILLIAM WALLACE AND ROBERT BRUCE. THROUGH ALL OF THEIR VICISSITUDES THEY HAVE REMAINED STUBBORNLY THEMSELVES.

PICTS, ROMANS AND SCOTS

EVIDENCE OF HUMAN SETTLEMENT IN SCOTLAND GOES
BACK AT LEAST FIVE THOUSAND YEARS, BEGINNING
WITH STONE AGE HUNTER-GATHERERS ON THE WEST
COAST WHO ATE QUANTITIES OF SHELLFISH AND
HUNTED THE RED DEER. IN DUE COURSE OTHER SET-
TLERS FOLLOWED. FARMING AND HERDING WERE
INTRODUCED, AND TOOLS AND WEAPONS OF BRONZE
AND IRON CAME INTO USE.

MYSTERIOUS SYMBOLS, CARVED ON THIS
STANDING STONE, ARE AMONG THE FEW REMAINS OF
PICTISH CULTURE. YET THIS PEOPLE PLAYED AN
IMPORTANT ROLE IN BRITISH HISTORY, RESISTING THE
ROMAN ADVANCE INTO SCOTLAND AND CONTROLLING
MOST OF THE TERRITORIES ABOVE THE FORTH-CLYDE
LINE UNTIL THE LATE 9TH CENTURY AD.

By the 1st century AD there were magnificent stone buildings and monuments in
Scotland, but although the houses, tombs,
stone circles and towers survive, no written
records exist to illuminate its peoples' origins,
history and customs. From the last millennium BC they are usually described as Celts,
but whether they invaded Scotland during
that period, and whether 'Celtic' even has any
meaning except as a linguistic or cultural
term, are matters still hotly debated.

In AD 43 the Romans crossed the Chan-
nel and began the conquest of Britain. We
know what happened when they marched
into Scotland because their offensive was
directed by Gnaeus Julius Agrippa, an outstanding soldier whose biography was written
by his son-in-law, the historian Tacitus. By
AD 81–2 the Romans had reached the Forth-
Clyde line, subduing the Celtic-speaking
Britons who lived below it. Beyond lay the
territory of tall, red-haired tribesmen whom
the Romans called Caledonians, and later
Picts (*Picti*, painted people). In 83 Agricola
advanced, establishing a powerful fortress on
the Tay and starting to build a line of forts to
pen the Caledonians into the Highlands. In
84 the Romans won a pitched battle at Mons
Graupius, somewhere in the north-east, the
army marched as far as the Moray Firth, and a
fleet sailed all the way round Scotland,
putting the Orkneys on the Roman map.

Despite his apparent success, Agricola was
recalled to Rome in 85 and the legions pulled
back to the Forth-Clyde line. After a visit to
Britain by the Emperor Hadrian in 122, permanent fortifications ('Hadrian's Wall') were

constructed from the Solway to the Tyne, just south of the present-day Anglo-Scottish border. The Romans had clearly switched from expansion to containment, which remained their policy for most of the following three centuries. The only exception was a brief period after 144, marked by the building of the turf Antonine Wall in an attempt to hold the Forth-Clyde line once more; when it was abandoned, Hadrian's Wall again became the Roman-Caledonian frontier.

By the 4th century the Roman Empire was in difficulties and more and more legions were being recalled from Britain. The Picts often struck out to the south in search of plunder, sometimes in alliance with two groups of seaborne raiders: the Scots, a Celtic people based in Northern Ireland, and the Germanic Angles and Saxons. The raiders soon became conquerors and settlers. The Angles and Saxons invaded southern Britain after the final departure of the Romans. At about the same time the Scots established the kingdom of Dalriada in the west of what is now Scotland, leaving the Picts in possession of the north. Below the Forth-Clyde line, the Celtic British continued to dominate the south-west (the kingdom of Strathclyde), but the Angles created a Northumbrian kingdom that took in the south-east as far as the Forth.

In time, these four groups fused to create the Scottish people. All four were converted to Christianity through the efforts of St Ninian (397) and St Columba, who came from Ireland and, having established himself on the island of Iona in 563, sent missionaries into Pictland.

The four kingdoms and their religion survived the onslaught of the Norse (Vikings), who terrorized most of Europe in the 8th and 9th centuries. Norse settlement and conquest of the Northern and Western Isles and the far north (Caithness and Sutherland) added yet another element to Scotland's racial mix. Politically the most significant outcome of the wars and invasions was the union of Scots and Picts in 843. Kenneth MacAlpin became the king of both peoples, and in a remarkably short time the Picts simply faded from the historical record. MacAlpin's realm of Alba, or Scotia, became the nucleus of a new northern kingdom and people.

A WELL-APPOINTED WHEEL-HOUSE AT JARLSHOF ON SHETLAND. THE WHEEL HOUSES (ARRANGED LIKE SEGMENTS ROUND A CENTRAL SPOKE) DATE FROM THE 8TH CENTURY AND ARE PART OF A SITE UNCOVERED IN 1890, WHEN A STORM BLEW AWAY SAND THAT HAD LONG COVERED A SETTLEMENT WHOSE HISTORY STRETCHED FROM THE NEOLITHIC TO VIKING TIMES.

ROME TRIUMPHS OVER THE BARBARIANS ON THIS RELIEF FROM THE ANTONINE WALL. BUT IN THE CASE OF SCOTLAND THE TRIUMPH WAS SHORT-LIVED: AFTER HOLDING THE LINE FOR TEN YEARS THE ROMANS WERE FORCED BACK TO HADRIAN'S WALL.

THE MEDIEVAL KINGDOM

SCOTIA BECAME SCOTLAND ONLY SLOWLY AND DOUBT-FULLY. THE SUCCESSORS OF KENNETH MACALPIN FOUGHT BLOODY BATTLES AGAINST THEIR NORSE AND ANGLO-SAXON NEIGHBOURS WHILE ALL TOO OFTEN DYING AT THE HANDS OF AMBITIOUS KINSMEN.

But in 1018 Malcolm II vanquished the Northumbrians and added Lothian to his kingdom; and in 1034 his grandson Duncan, who already ruled Strathclyde, inherited the Scottish throne and incorporated the ancient British realm into his northern kingdom. Its southern border was established along a line not very different from the present-day border, but the territories conquered by the Norse continued to owe allegiance to Scandinavian kings; the Western Isles were acquired from Norway only in 1266, and the Orkneys and Shetlands became Scottish – in name though not in culture – even later, as part of a marriage settlement in 1468–72.

Meanwhile Scotland's difficult relationship with her larger southern neighbour was taking shape. Following the Viking invasions, a single English state replaced the rival Anglo-Saxon kingdoms, and as early as 921 the Scottish king Constantine II found it necessary to acknowledge Edward the Elder of England as his overlord. English suzerainty was twice confirmed during the 10th century, with especially picturesque symbolism in 973, when Kenneth II of Scotland and seven other British rulers plied the oars on the River Dee while the English king Edgar sat at the helm. Overlordship was of limited practical significance, but English intervention was probably decisive in one famous episode of Scottish his-

THE NOBLE RUINS OF MELROSE ABBEY. FOUNDED IN 1136 BY CISTERCIAN MONKS FROM RIELVAUX IN YORKSHIRE, MELROSE ENJOYED ROYAL FAVOUR AND FLOURISHED DESPITE SUFFERING IN THE ANGLO-SCOTTISH WARS AND BEING REBUILT IN THE 15TH CENTURY. IT FELL INTO RUIN AFTER BEING RAVAGED BY ENGLISH SOLDIERS AND SCOTS PROTESTANTS.

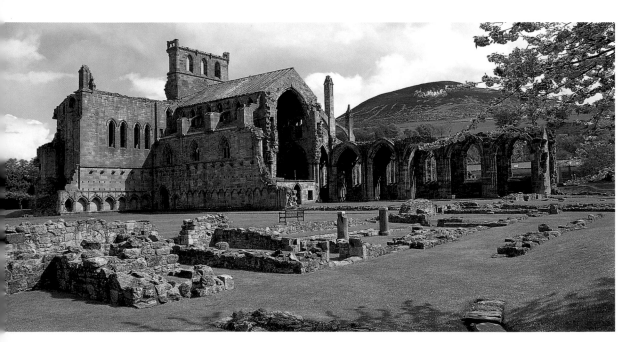

tory. In 1040 King Duncan was dispatched by one of his relatives, Macbeth, who made himself king; Shakespeare turned the usurpation and its sequel into a tragedy of ambition, guilt and swift retribution, but the historical Macbeth reigned for fourteen years before Siward, Earl of Northumbria, backed an invasion in which Macbeth was defeated and, three years later, killed by Duncan's son Malcolm III of Canmore.

Macbeth was the last ruler in the established Celtic tradition. Under Malcolm and his successors, Scotland was transformed from a Celtic clan society to a feudal society of the kind introduced in England after the Norman Conquest of 1066. In traditional Celtic society the High King had little control over the kings or chiefs he ruled; they were men of power, usually kinsmen and potential rivals, especially since royal authority was weakened by tanistry – the suc-

DAVID I OF SCOTLAND AND HIS GRANDSON MALCOLM IV; ILLUMINATED INITIAL FROM THE CHARTER OF KELSO ABBEY. DAVID WAS BROUGHT UP AT THE ENGLISH COURT AND CREATED EARL OF HUNTINGDON BY HENRY I; WHEN HE BECAME KING IN 1124 HE PROMOTED ANGLO-NORMAN IMMIGRATION AND NORMAN-STYLE FEUDALISM.

cession to the throne of adult brothers or cousins rather than royal children. Feudalism meant primogeniture (inheritance by the eldest child) and a pyramidal social structure, based on land-holding and military service, with the king at its apex; and in immediate practical terms it meant a more advanced military technology based on stone castles and mounted and armoured knights.

Scottish feudalism was largely established under Norman influence. This was first felt thanks to Malcolm III's wife, Margaret – paradoxically, since she was a member of the Anglo-Saxon ruling family displaced by the Conquest. Under Margaret and her three sons, notably David I (1124–53), many Anglo-Normans settled in Scotland, including families such as the Balliols, Bruces and Stewarts who would play crucial roles in her history. A new, Norman-French-speaking aristocracy emerged, while a form of northern English increasingly became the common speech of the south and east, eventually confining Gaelic to the Highlands. Margaret also worked to eliminate Celtic practices from the Church and replace them by Roman orthodoxy – to such effect that she was canonized as St Margaret.

The 'bloodless Norman Conquest' of Scotland did not prevent her kings from enthusiastically going to war with her southern neighbour, though few were more successful than William the Lion, captured in 1174 and, like so many of his predecessors, compelled to do homage to the English king; fortunately for the Scots, King Richard of England was desperate for crusading money and allowed William to buy his way out of feudal servitude. In the 13th century, hostilities between the two kingdoms abated, only to flare up again in a crisis which threatened the very survival of Scotland as an independent kingdom.

WARS OF INDEPENDENCE

THE THREAT TO SCOTLAND'S INDEPENDENCE WAS BROUGHT ABOUT BY THE EXTINCTION OF THE ROYAL LINE. ALEXANDER III'S ONLY SON DIED IN 1284, AND THE ALREADY ELDERLY KING'S ONLY DIRECT DESCENDANT WAS HIS GRANDDAUGHTER MARGARET, A CHILD IN NORWAY.

Alexander himself died two years later, and in 1289 a match was announced between Margaret and Prince Edward, eldest son of Edward I of England. But 'the Maid of Norway' died on the voyage to Scotland and, for better or worse, the chance of peacefully uniting the Scottish and English crowns was lost. There was now no clear successor, and members of several leading families were able to put forward plausible claims to the throne. To avoid a civil war, it was agreed that Edward I of England should be asked to arbitrate. It was a dangerous request, since Edward had proved himself a formidable and ruthless warrior as a crusader in the East and as the conqueror of Wales. Predictably, Edward insisted that the Scots must first recognize him as the feudal Paramount Lord of Scotland. The over-eager candidates stifled their doubts and accepted his terms. Having declared that one of their number, John Balliol, was the rightful king of Scotland, Edward quickly demonstrated that he intended to be overlord in more than name, summoning and dismissing his royal vassal with such arrogance that even the pliable Balliol was driven to revolt; the treaty he made with the French king Philip IV marked the beginning of a Franco-Scottish 'Auld Alliance' against England that would be renewed again and again over the next three centuries.

Edward reacted swiftly and brutally. A single campaign in 1296 crushed the Scots. Balliol was deposed, and among other treasures the

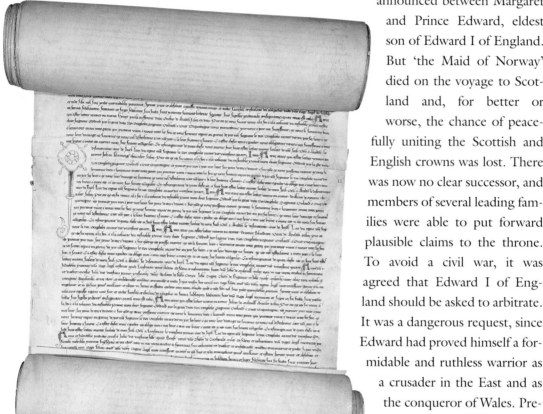

DISLOYAL LOYALTY. THE RAGMAN ROLLS CONTAIN THE SIGNATURES OF TWO THOUSAND SCOTS NOTABLES, AFFIXED TO A DECLARATION OF FEALTY TO EDWARD I OF ENGLAND. HUMILIATING BUT PRUDENT, THIS ACT OF SUBMISSION WAS MADE AT BERWICK IN 1296, AFTER EDWARD HAD CRUSHED AND DETHRONED KING JOHN BALLIOL.

English carried off the Stone of Scone (or Stone of Destiny) on which Scottish kings were consecrated. At Berwick, two thousand chastened Scottish notables swore an oath of fealty to King Edward. Not all the Scottish lords submitted, but the most effective resistance was organized by a young man who was at best a member of the minor gentry and by some accounts an outlaw. William Wallace raised a popular army, in September 1297 cut to pieces an English force at Stirling Bridge, and for a few months effectively ruled in John Balliol's name as Guardian of Scotland. Then Edward himself, back from the French wars, marched north and crushed Wallace's army at Falkirk. Wallace fled, but many of the Scottish lords (who had generally refused to help him, apparently because of his inferior birth) remained in arms. At last, in 1305, the remaining rebel stronghold, Stirling Castle, surrendered, and when Wallace re-emerged he was immediately betrayed, given a mockery of a trial and put to a hideous death.

Just when Edward's triumph seemed assured, Scotland found her greatest leader in Robert Bruce. Like almost every other Scottish lord, he was by no means a patriot in the modern sense, having changed sides several times. Resentment of foreign rule and the chance of glory and plunder were motives for rebellion; but thanks to the complexities of the feudal system, many Scots held lands in both Scotland and England, so that any unswerving allegiance came at a price in one country or the other, and when the English king seemed to be winning it was tempting to play safe and come to terms with him. Rivalries between great families also created shifting loyalties, and it was a long-running family feud that finally determined Bruce's fate. In 1306, during a meeting to negotiate with John Comyn the Red, Bruce lost his temper and stabbed his old enemy. The killing took place in a church, and the combination of murder and sacrilege left Bruce with no option but to seize power or perish.

THE STONE OF DESTINY, OR STONE OF SCONE, WAS BELIEVED TO BE OF GREAT ANTIQUITY AND WAS USED DURING THE CORONATION OF SCOTTISH MONARCHS FROM DALRIADIC TIMES OR EARLIER. EDWARD I CARRIED IT OFF IN 1296; IT THEN REMAINED IN WESTMINSTER ABBEY, EXCEPT FOR A FEW MONTHS IN 1950 WHEN IT WAS TAKEN BY SCOTTISH NATIONALISTS, UNTIL ITS RETURN TO SCOTLAND IN 1998.

In the image, handwritten annotations read: "K. Robert (9) Bruce and his second wyff" and "Robert dochter to the Earle of Ulster in Irland"

SCOTLAND'S CHAMPION. ROBERT BRUCE, GRASPING THE ROYAL STANDARD, AND HIS SECOND WIFE; FROM SETON'S ARMORIAL CRESTS. THE PORTRAITS ARE EVIDENTLY IMAGINARY, REFLECTING LATER FASHIONS IN APPEARANCE AND DRESS. ENSHRINED AS A NATIONAL HERO, 'THE BRUCE' HAS LARGELY LIVED DOWN HIS NONE-TOO-PATRIOTIC PAST.

Hastily crowned king, Bruce rode and fought tirelessly, experiencing many vicissitudes including periods as a fugitive when, legend has it, he learned the need to persist in his efforts from the example of a spider spinning and re-spinning its broken web. More pertinently, he devised an effective hit-and-run strategy that wore down his English and Scottish enemies. He was helped by the fact that Edward I's successor, Edward II, was not a warrior by temperament and was constantly at odds with his own barons. By 1314 Bruce was conducting devastating raids into the north of England, and the commander of the last English-held fortress, Stirling Castle, had agreed to surrender unless a relief arrived within a stipulated time. A dilatory Edward II marched on Scotland with a formidable army to relieve the castle, and on 24 June 1314 the Scots led by Bruce won their greatest victory at Bannockburn, just outside Stirling, where a few thousand spearmen trapped a formidable English army in a neck of swampy land and slaughtered it. King Edward escaped with some difficulty, fled to Dunbar, and hastily took ship for England.

The battle of Bannockburn has rightly been seen as a turning point in Scottish fortunes. But even after his humiliating defeat Edward II could not bring himself to recognize that Scotland was an independent kingdom and that its ruler was not a rebellious vassal but King Robert I. For his own reasons Pope John XXII took the same view as the English king, and in 1320 his stance elicited a Scottish protest, the Declaration of Arbroath, whose eloquence has rung down the ages. In a still-feudal world, its Latin phrases sounded the authentic note of modern nationhood: 'as long as even a hundred of us remain alive, we shall never on any conditions submit to English rule. In truth it is not for glory, or riches, or honours that we fight, but for freedom, which no honest man will give up except with life itself.' Sporadic, futile campaigns went on even after the unlucky Edward was deposed and murdered, but the English finally accepted the inevitable by signing the Treaty of Northampton in 1328. Scotland's independence was

acknowledged, and a marriage was arranged between Bruce's heir and an English princess.

But Scotland's history remained turbulent. Bruce died in 1329, leaving his five-year-old son to become David II. Three years later Edward Balliol, son of the Scottish king whom Edward I had humiliated, managed to seize the throne. He was soon driven out, but he returned with the help of an English army which won a significant victory at Halidon Hill (1333). This served notice on the Scots that the armies of Edward III were far more formidable than those of his father; but in spite of the warning, and England's patent superiority in manpower and other resources, the Scots continued to make war on the old enemy for centuries, exhibiting an astounding but ultimately tragic combination of valour, pride and folly.

All of these were present in David II when, grown to manhood, he reclaimed his kingdom and invaded England in support of his French allies. In 1346 David's army was shattered at Neville's Cross, and the recently returned king spent the following eleven years in the Tower of London until his countrymen ransomed him.

Dying childless, David was succeeded by Robert II, whose father had married Robert Bruce's daughter Margaret. Robert was the first of a new, long-lived, but hardly happy dynasty: the Stewarts.

A DECEPTIVE AMITY. EDWARD III OF ENGLAND AND SCOTLAND'S DAVID II SHAKE HANDS WITHIN AN ILLUMINATED INITIAL. THEY WERE BROTHERS-IN-LAW (DAVID HAD MARRIED EDWARD'S SISTER), BUT DAVID'S ADHERENCE TO THE AULD ALLIANCE WITH FRANCE LED TO A SCOTTISH DISASTER AT NEVILLE'S CROSS (1346).

STEWART CALAMITIES

FOR ALMOST FOUR CENTURIES THE FORTUNES OF SCOT-
LAND WERE BOUND UP WITH THOSE OF THE STRANGELY
UNLUCKY HOUSE OF STEWART, WHICH REIGNED FROM
1371 TO 1688. THE STEWARTS WERE DESCENDED FROM
BRETON ADVENTURERS, THE FITZALANS, WHO
MIGRATED FROM ENGLAND TO SCOTLAND UNDER
DAVID I, ACQUIRING THEIR SURNAME FROM THEIR
OFFICE AS HEREDITARY STEWARDS TO THE KING.

JAMES II, LIKE SO MANY OF THE STEWARTS,
EXPERIENCED THE VAGARIES OF FORTUNE. AS A BOY HE
ATTENDED THE 'BLACK DINNER' AT WHICH THE
DOUGLAS BROTHERS WERE SLAIN; LATER HE HIMSELF
WOULD MURDER A DOUGLAS. SEEMINGLY POWERFUL
AND SECURE, HE WAS KILLED AT THE SIEGE OF
ROXBURGH CASTLE WHEN A CANNON EXPLODED.

Neither Robert II nor his son Robert III was a strong king, and during their reigns a pattern of lawlessness and violence, already well-established during the wars for independence, became even more marked. One legacy of the wars was reiving – cross-border plundering and burning by Scots and English freebooters whose loyalties, if any, were not to a king but to great families such as the Douglases and Percies. The clans of the Highlands and Islands were also wild, fierce and lawless in their hatreds. But even in central Scotland, murder and mayhem broke out whenever the king was weak or a minor, as lords great and small formed factions, engaged in bloody fights, plotted assassinations, and kidnapped royal children in order to gain control of the government. Violence bred counter-violence, and the reassertion of royal authority, when it came, always involved rough justice and ruthless shedding of blood.

A long period of firm, good government was clearly what Scotland needed. But for over two centuries this was prevented through a series of dynastic accidents that repeatedly undermined royal authority by bringing a child to the throne. The calamities that befell the Stewarts were so many and unrelenting that they can be made to sound almost fiction-ally ludicrous. Robert III (1390–1406) was disabled, and in that rough age his inability to lead an army in person was a serious disadvantage. A reign filled with anarchy, civil wars and conspiracies culminated in the king's decision to send his son James to France, where he would be safe from Robert's ambitious brother, the Earl of Albany. But the ship was intercepted by the English and the twelve-year-old Prince James became a prisoner in the Tower of London. He almost immediately became King James I (1406–37), since his father died (it is said of grief)

after hearing the news. In England, James developed into an accomplished poet while Albany ruled Scotland, preserving a fragile calm until his death in 1420. Then law and order broke down again until 1424, when James I was at last able to return from his eighteen-year exile.

Despite his inexperience he proved an able ruler, but in 1437 he was assassinated as part of a plot within his own family. His six-year-old heir, James II (1437–60), survived a turbulent childhood and youth, filled with macabre scenes of treachery and violence, and emerged as master of the country by committing comparable acts of treachery and violence. He seemed well-placed to intervene with profit in the first phase of England's civil war, the Wars of the Roses, and laid siege to Roxburgh – but was killed there when one of his own cannons exploded beside him. His nine-year-old son, James III (1460–88), lived to become a notably unpopular ruler. He broke the MacDonald Lords of the Isles, who had emerged as a power in the west following the end of Norwegian rule; but when he attempted to wage war on England, his barons refused to fight and hanged his favourites instead. Eventually James was defeated in battle by his rebellious subjects and murdered as he fled.

James IV (1488–1513) inherited the throne when he was a relatively mature sixteen; greatly gifted and popular, he ruled over a prosperous people, but went to war with England and fell at the most disastrous of all the Scots' battles, Flodden Field, where the flower of Scotland's fighting men, nobles as well as commoners, perished. His one-year-old heir, James V (1513–42), had the same sort of dangerous childhood as his predecessors but was much less popular than his father; after his army was defeated by the English at Solway Moss, he seems to have died of sheer discouragement, perhaps compounded by the birth of a female heir, later known to history as Mary, Queen of Scots.

MONS MEG. THIS FORMIDABLE, FOUR-METRE-LONG GUN, NOW IN EDINBURGH CASTLE, IS SCOTLAND'S LARGEST MEDIEVAL ARTILLERY PIECE. IT WAS A GIFT TO JAMES II FROM THE DUKE OF BURGUNDY, WHOSE DOMINIONS INCLUDED MONS WHERE IT WAS MANUFACTURED. JAMES MADE GOOD USE OF ARTILLERY TO QUELL HIS REBELLIOUS SUBJECTS.

A CROWN CAPTURED: AN ILLUSTRATION FROM A CONTEMPORARY DESCRIPTION OF THE BATTLE OF FLODDEN IN 1513. JAMES IV LED A LARGE, WELL-EQUIPPED ARMY INTO NORTHUMBERLAND WHILE HENRY VIII OF ENGLAND WAS INVADING FRANCE, ONLY TO BE DEFEATED AND KILLED BY A SCRATCH FORCE COMMANDED BY THE EARL OF SURREY.

THE SCOTTISH REFORMATION

IN THE 16TH CENTURY, NEW CONFLICTS DISTURBED THE ALREADY TURBULENT, FACTION-RIDDEN CONDITION OF SCOTLAND. THE PROTESTANT REFORMATION, BEGUN IN 1517 BY THE GERMAN MONK MARTIN LUTHER, ATTRACTED FOLLOWERS IN MOST PARTS OF EUROPE AND BECAME DOMINANT IN A NUMBER OF STATES.

Initially a reaction against undoubted abuses in the Catholic Church, it rapidly assumed a separate character, with distinctive doctrines, forms of church organization, and views as to the function of the priesthood and the role of the laity. Among the most obvious manifestations of the 'Reformed Religion' were the repudiation of papal authority, plainer forms of worship, hostility to 'idolatry' (sacred images and the cult of the Virgin and the saints) and, as part of an emphasis on individual religious experience, having the Bible available to all who could read by translating it into the native tongue of each country.

In time, Protestantism would make an enormous impact on the Scottish way of life, and 'the Kirk' (the Church) in its Presbyterian form would become a national institution. But although its first martyr, Patrick Hamilton, was burned as a heretic in 1528, it was slow to take hold. By contrast, Henry VIII of England broke with the Pope in the 1530s and made himself head of the national church, acts that did not entail an immediate transition to Protestantism but were enough to brand the king as a heretic. This was certainly the view taken by James V's privy council and the Scottish clergy in 1541; consequently they refused to allow the king to keep an appointment to meet Henry at York – a snub that led directly to war and James's defeat at Solway Moss – and, arguably, his death, the accession of the six-day-old Mary ('Queen of Scots') and the momentous events that followed.

War, politics and religion now became thoroughly enmeshed. Henry VIII proposed a match between his infant heir, Edward, and Scotland's child queen. When the Scots rejected the idea, Henry began a 'Rough Wooing' to coerce them by regular, punitively

ONE OF THE MOST COLOURFUL STEWART KINGS, JAMES V WAS A GREAT AMORIST AND ENJOYED MINGLING WITH THE COMMON PEOPLE IN DISGUISE. A ZEALOUS CHAMPION OF CATHOLICISM AGAINST THE PROTESTANT REFORMERS, HE WENT TO WAR WITH THE HERETICAL HENRY VIII OF ENGLAND, WAS DEFEATED AT SOLWAY MOSS AND DIED WHEN STILL ONLY THIRTY.

destructive invasions culminating in a major English victory at the battle of Pinkie and a temporary occupation of south-eastern Scotland. Anti-English feeling was inevitably identified with anti-Protestantism, making the Reformed Religion suspect in the eyes of many Scots, despite the sympathy created in 1546 by the burning of a new and prominent martyr, George Wishart. Moreover the Rough Wooing failed in all its objectives. It strengthened the position of Mary of Guise, the French mother of Mary, Queen of Scots, who seized the opportunity to invite French troops into the country and send her daughter to France to be the bride of the Dauphin.

With events apparently moving in her favour, Mary of Guise was able to take power directly, becoming Regent of Scotland in 1554. Then the completeness of her triumph began to work against her, as the Scottish nobility increasingly resented her ever-growing entourage of French officials and the apparently permanent presence of foreign troops in the country. Policy and religion combined to produce an opposition backed by wealth and force. In 1557 a group of nobles banded together and, calling themselves the Lords of the Congregation, publicly embraced Protestant principles. Protestant exiles, notably the fiery John Knox, returned to Scotland and stirred up popular feeling. The civil war that followed was influenced by the accession of Elizabeth I of England in 1558: Scotland's southern neighbour became an unmistakably Protestant country, and English aid was welcomed by the Protestant and anti-French party. After the death of the Regent in June 1560, her Scottish and French followers were rapidly defeated and in July the Treaty of Edinburgh provided for the withdrawal of all foreign troops.

Within a month, the Scottish Parliament had broken with Rome and made Protestantism the established religion, based on a Confession of Faith written by John Knox. Meanwhile Mary, Queen of Scots, had married the Dauphin and become queen of France; but in December 1560 her husband died and she no longer had a role to play abroad. The following year, Scotland's devoutly Catholic queen returned to face the devoutly Protestant leaders of her people.

JOHN KNOX HARANGUING MARY, QUEEN OF SCOTS. SINCE MARY WAS NOT ONLY A CATHOLIC BUT A WOMAN, KNOX RESENTED HER ROYAL AUTHORITY AND USED HIS POSITION OF HIGH INFLUENCE TO POINT OUT THE ERROR OF HER WAYS AT GREAT LENGTH. MARY STOOD FIRM BUT HAD TO ACCEPT PROTESTANT DOMINATION IN SCOTLAND.

THE PROTESTANT PREACHER George Wishart was burned for heresy in 1546, an event commemorated by this naïve but effective print. Wishart's death also enabled his assistant, John Knox, to become the main Scottish spokesman for Protestantism.

THE QUEEN OF SCOTS

MARY, QUEEN OF SCOTS, WAS A CONTROVERSIAL FIGURE DURING HER LIFETIME AND HAS DIVIDED HISTORIANS AND STUDENTS OF HISTORY EVER SINCE. HER ADMIRERS SEE HER AS A ROMANTIC ICON – A WOMAN WHO FOLLOWED HER HEART IN AN AGE WHEN COLDLY CALCULATING MARRIAGE ALLIANCES WERE THE RULE, AND BEHAVED WITH FLEXIBILITY AND TOLERANCE WHEN CONFRONTED WITH CONFLICTING FANATICISMS.

Others believe that the undoubted failures of her career were easily avoidable, and that Mary brought about her own ruin by her shallowness and short-sighted opportunism. On all of these matters, the jury is still out.

Although she made an indelible impression on the world's imagination, Mary's role in Scottish history was actually small and brief. At the age of five she was shipped off to France, where she grew up at the court and at fifteen married the Dauphin Francis. A secret agreement stipulated that if she died without issue the Scottish crown would pass to her husband; so contemporary Scots' fears of French domination were well founded. In the event it was Francis who died, and Mary who returned in August 1561 to begin a reign that had technically existed since her birth and would last for less than seven years.

Though herself a Catholic, Mary had to accept the existing Protestant settlement, including the persecution of her fellow-Catholics. This was an uneasy situation at a time when state and church were normally united in enforcing a single religious faith. Moreover foreign policy was complicated by the fact that Mary was the presumptive heir of Queen Elizabeth of England, now the natural ally of a Protestant Scotland. Such dynastic considerations made the question of whom Mary should marry an especially delicate one. However, instead of making a royal match, she chose her young cousin and closest relative, Henry Stewart, Lord Darnley. Avoiding dynastic difficulties seems to have been a less important motive than simple personal preference; but the arrogant and erratic Darnley rapidly proved to be an unsuitable husband with ambitions to become king rather than consort. A disenchanted Mary relied increasingly on the support and advice of her personal retainers, and both Darnley and the Protestant nobles became jealously suspicious of an Italian musician, David Rizzio, who served as the queen's French secretary. On 9 March 1566, at Edinburgh, Darnley and other lords burst into a room in Holyrood Palace and stabbed Rizzio to death. The queen, six-months' pregnant, was either present or close at

MARY, QUEEN OF SCOTS, IS MORE REGAL IF LESS BEAUTIFUL, IN THIS MINIATURE BY HILLIARD THAN HER POPULAR LEGEND WOULD HAVE IT. THE MINGLING OF LOVE, POLITICS, RELIGION AND MURDER IN HER CAREER HAS MADE HER ENDLESSLY FASCINATING TO HISTORIANS, BUT FINAL JUDGEMENTS ABOUT HER ARE IMPOSSIBLE IN THE ABSENCE OF KEY FACTS.

hand when the murder was committed.

Having little choice, Mary allowed herself to be formally reconciled with her husband, and in June 1566 gave birth to his child, the future James VI. But the months that followed were filled with rumours of divorce and obscure negotiations whose details and significance have proved impossible to disentangle. Then, on 10 January 1567, an explosion destroyed the house in Kirk o'Field, Edinburgh, where Darnley was recovering from smallpox. Darnley was unhurt, but his body was found in a field outside the house, strangled. The mystery was never solved, but there was strong circumstantial evidence to suggest that the murders were the work of the Earl of Bothwell, who had become closely associated with Mary. Whether or not the queen knew of the scheme has always been hotly debated.

THE EARL OF BOTHWELL, JAMES HEPBURN, IS AS CONTROVERSIAL A FIGURE AS MARY. HE WAS ALMOST CERTAINLY A PARTY TO THE DEATH OF THE QUEEN'S FIRST HUSBAND, DARNLEY. WHETHER HE AND MARY WERE LOVERS OR POLITICAL ALLIES, OR WHETHER MARY WAS FORCED TO MARRY HIM, ARE UNRESOLVED ISSUES. MINIATURE OF THE FLEMISH SCHOOL.

The crisis of the reign developed very rapidly. Bothwell was tried for murder and acquitted. On 24 April he abducted Mary; on 7 May he divorced his wife; on 15 May he and Mary were married in a Protestant ceremony. Once more, the motives of the partners concerned are problematic. Was Mary in love with Bothwell, consolidating a political alliance, or acting partly under duress? Whatever the truth may be, the outcome was disastrous. The marriage was universally regarded as a scandal. A noble opposition formed, and when Mary and Bothwell met them at Carberry on 15 June, the royal forces melted away, Mary surrendered, and Bothwell fled abroad, to end his days miserably in a Norwegian prison.

Mary herself was confined to Loch Leven Castle and compelled to abdicate in favour of her son. Eight months later she managed to escape and raise a new force, but in May 1568 she was defeated at Langside and fled to England.

At first it seemed possible that Elizabeth would intervene to restore Mary. But at an English court of enquiry, the new regent, Moray, produced a casket holding letters from Mary to Bothwell that incriminated her in the murder of Darnley. Historians tend to question the authenticity of these 'Casket Letters', brought to light at such a convenient moment; but since the originals no longer exist, the facts can never be ascertained. The inquiry ended without reaching a definite decision, and Mary remained in England for eighteen years as a guest and captive until, as the focus of Catholic plots against Elizabeth, she was executed at Fotheringay on 8 February 1587.

COVENANTS AND KINGS

WHEN MARY, QUEEN OF SCOTS, ABDICATED IN 1567, SHE WAS SUC-CEEDED BY HER ONE-YEAR-OLD SON, JAMES VI. THE FAMILIAR ROUND OF KIDNAPPINGS, ASSASSINATIONS AND FAMILY FEUDS WAS RESUMED DURING JAMES'S MINORITY, AND THE TERRORS OF HIS CHILDHOOD – OR PERHAPS HIS PRE-NATAL EXPERI-ENCE OF RIZZIO'S MURDER – HELPED TO MAKE HIM A NOTABLY ECCENTRIC, SHAMBLING INDIVIDUAL WHOSE FEAR OF ASSASSINATION CAUSED HIM TO WEAR GROTESQUELY PADDED DOUBLETS.

Nevertheless James was shrewd enough except when it came to overspending and handsome young men, and once he came of age he was remarkably successful in re-establishing royal authority. This even extended to Scotland's militant and high-principled Reformed Church. By the 1580s Scottish Protestantism had developed a presbyterian form of church government, run by ministers and lay elders through ecclesiastical courts; the highest court was the General Assembly, presided over by a Moderator. James disapproved of this essentially egalitarian system, but although he succeeded in imposing episcopacy – archbishops and bishops – on the Church of Scotland, services remained free of the ritual elements characteristic of, for example, the Church of England.

James's policies were largely conditioned by his determination to inherit the English throne from the ageing Elizabeth, which prevented him from protesting strongly even when his mother was executed. On Elizabeth's death in 1603 he duly became James I of England as well as James VI of Scotland; from this time the dynasty is usually called Stuart rather than Stewart. The two countries – old enemies – now had the same king, but in other respects they remained separate. Neither Scots nor English favoured James's plans for a formal union, but with the same royal authority operating on both sides of the border, the lawless reiving way of life began to be brought under control.

James had a good deal of trouble with his English parliaments. His son, Charles I, higher-minded and less flexible, experienced even greater difficulties, which he tried to overcome by living within his means and doing without parliament. But his attempt to impose a new

A RIOT IN CHURCH. ON 23 JULY 1637, WHEN THE DEAN OF ST GILES CATHEDRAL BEGAN TO READ FROM THE UNPOPULAR NEW SERVICE-BOOK INTRODUCED BY CHARLES I, A WOMAN NAMED JENNY GEDDES IS SAID TO HAVE FLUNG A STOOL AT HIM. A RIOT BROKE OUT, WITH MOMENTOUS, LONG-TERM CONSEQUENCES FOR BOTH SCOTLAND AND ENGLAND.

THE NATIONAL COVENANT OF 1638. SOME 300,000 SCOTS ARE BELIEVED TO HAVE SIGNED THIS DOCUMENT OR ONE OF THE COPIES CIRCULATED THROUGHOUT THE LOWLANDS. A DEFENCE OF SCOTTISH RIGHTS AGAINST CHARLES I'S POLICY TOWARDS THE CHURCH OF SCOTLAND LITURGY, THE COVENANT LONG REMAINED A FUNDAMENTAL DOCUMENT OF SCOTTISH PRESBYTERIANISM.

prayer book on Scotland ruined his plans. In July 1637 there was a riot when the new forms were used for the first time in St Giles' Cathedral, Edinburgh, and, in a great upsurge of religious and patriotic feeling, hundreds of thousands of Scots put their signatures to a National Covenant that pledged them to defend 'the true religion'. Charles's attempts to use force were defeated and, by bankrupting him, brought on fateful confrontations that culminated in the Civil War between the king and the English Parliament.

The Scots intervened in England's Civil War on their own terms. In 1643 the English Parliamentarians signed a Solemn League and Covenant committing them to Presbyterianism in return for Scottish military assistance; the Scottish royalists took up arms, brilliantly led by the Marquis of Montrose, but were ultimately defeated. When the war in England

THE COVENANTING GRINDSTONE. THE CARTOON DESCRIBES THE PLIGHT OF CHARLES II IN 1650, UNRECOGNIZED BY REPUBLICAN ENGLAND AND COMPELLED TO COME TO TERMS WITH PRESBYTERIAN SCOTLAND. CHARLES ACCEPTED THE COVENANT, BUT THE ROYALISTS AND SCOTS WERE DEFEATED; WHEN HE WAS FINALLY RESTORED IN 1660, HE FORGOT HIS OATHS AND PERSECUTED THE COVENANTERS.

was lost, the king surrendered to the Scots, who handed him over to their allies. But the Solemn League was frustrated by radical new developments in England, including the emergence of Oliver Cromwell at the head of the powerful 'New Model' parliamentary army, which secured the execution of Charles I and the establishment of a republican Commonwealth. As a result, the Scots turned to Charles's exiled son, who was crowned Charles II of Scotland after a compulsory, patently insincere conversion to Presbyterianism. Neither side benefited from the arrangement. In 1650–51 the Scots armies were crushed by Cromwell at Dunbar and Worcester, Charles fled abroad again, and Scotland was occupied by English troops.

Scotland welcomed the collapse of the Commonwealth and the Restoration of Charles II in 1660. But the religious settlement was not as Charles had promised. The Scottish Church again came under the authority of bishops, and when the most uncompromising Covenanters refused to conform, holding meetings in hillside conventicles, they were harshly persecuted. Some took up arms, despite the superiority of the government forces, and the period became branded on the popular memory as 'the Killing Time'.

Conflicts in England were more complex, strenuously testing Charles II's ability to survive. Charles triumphed in the end, but his Catholic brother and successor, James VII and II, was less shrewd. His three-year reign ended when the English political elite turned to his Protestant daughter Mary and her Dutch husband, William of Orange. James fled into exile and the Scots followed the English example by offering the crown to William and Mary on terms that produced the kind of government and church desired by the majority.

THE JACOBITE CAUSE

THE ACCESSION OF WILLIAM AND MARY MARKED THE BEGINNING OF A NEW CONSTITUTIONAL ORDER IN SCOTLAND AND ENGLAND, AND WITHIN A GENERATION THERE WERE FURTHER DEVELOPMENTS THAT THRUST THE 17TH-CENTURY STRUGGLES, BETWEEN SCOTS AND ENGLISH AND CROWN AND PARLIAMENT, FIRMLY INTO THE PAST.

Scotland and England were merged by the 1707 Act of Union, and in 1714 the elector of Hanover became George I of Great Britain. As Catholics, James VII and his heirs were barred from the succession, and there was to be no second restoration of the house of Stuart.

Yet the fallen dynasty commanded a surprisingly persistent loyalty, and its efforts to regain the throne acquired a romantic aura within just a few years of their failure. The followers of James VII and his son 'James VIII', also known as the Old Pretender, were called Jacobites, a word derived from the Latin for James, *Jacobus*. True Jacobites were believers in the divine right of kings and the inviolable hereditary principle; but there were many others whose Jacobitism was motivated by a more or less serious disaffection with the existing authorities. As time went on, Jacobitism became for many a sentimental indulgence, mainly consisting of coded toasts to 'the king over the water'; events were to show that, when the call came, most 18th-century English Jacobites were not prepared to take up the sword.

THE FIRST JACOBITE HERO WAS JOHN GRAHAM OF CLAVERHOUSE, CREATED VISCOUNT DUNDEE BY JAMES VII FOR SUPPRESSING THE REBELLIOUS COVENANTERS. HIS RUTHLESSNESS WAS FORGOTTEN, AND HE BECAME 'BONNIE DUNDEE', WHEN HE DEFIED THE SCOTTISH CONVENTION THAT DEPOSED JAMES, RAISED AN ARMY, AND DIED GLORIOUSLY IN THE MOMENT OF VICTORY AT KILLIECRANKIE.

For this, the Stuarts could only rely on some – by no means all – of the Highland clans. Old loyalties stirred their blood and their valour was prodigious. But the appeal of Jacobitism also had much to do with their love of raiding and plunder and anarchic independence; and many also came out because they resented the ascendancy of the Campbells, whose chiefs, the Dukes of Argyll, had consistently backed the Covenanting and Hanoverian causes. To Lowlanders the clansmen seemed no better than lawless savages; unless led with great elan, they were reluctant to venture far from their own territories or to take part in protracted campaigns, often simply drifting away when there were no battles to be fought.

Nevertheless it was clansmen who backed the first Jacobite rising, undertaken at almost the moment the crown was lost. James Gra-

LOYAL TOASTS WERE DRUNK TO 'THE KING ACROSS THE WATER', WIDELY ENOUGH TO GIVE RISE TO A TYPE OF WARE KNOWN AS A JACOBITE GLASS. SOME EXAMPLES CARRIED PORTRAITS OF JAMES II AND VII OR THE OLD OR YOUNG PRETENDER; MOST WERE MORE DISCREETLY DECORATED WITH JACOBITE SYMBOLS SUCH AS ROSES, THISTLES AND OAK LEAVES.

ham of Claverhouse, Viscount Dundee, had served James VII well in suppressing the Covenanters, for whom he was 'Bluidie Clavers'. Present in Edinburgh when the Convention of the Estates decided for William and against James, he was proclaimed a rebel, made a rapid escape, and raised a force of MacDonalds, Camerons, Macleans and Stewarts to fight for the deposed king. His gallant, energetic effort culminated in July 1689 at the pass of Killiecrankie, where the outnumbered Highlanders smashed a much larger government force. But Claverhouse was killed in the melée, and a check at Dunkeld was enough to persuade the leaderless clansmen to go back to their homes. The following year James VII was driven from Ireland, leaving the Williamites triumphant in all three kingdoms.

They remained so for twenty years, but fear of the still-untamed clans led to an infamous episode. The government required all the rebellious clans to take an oath of allegiance by 1 January 1692. By accident rather than design, MacIain of Glencoe arrived late at Inverary, and although the oath was administered his failure was seized upon as an opportunity to cow the clans by eliminating his small but troublesome branch of the MacDonalds. Two companies of Campbells were billeted on the Glencoe MacDonalds, who treated their unwanted guests hospitably enough; then, on 13 February, the soldiers began to carry out their orders 'to put all to the sword under seventy'. As a military operation it was poorly executed, but the results were horrible enough. Hindered by a snowstorm, the troops killed about forty MacDonalds, including a few women and children; several hundred managed escape through the passes, which other government forces failed to block in time, but many of the fugitives died from exposure in the severe weather.

THE GATES OF TRAQUAIR WILL REMAIN SHUT, IT IS SAID, UNTIL A STUART SITS ON THE THRONE AGAIN. THIS FINE HOUSE HAS BEEN OWNED BY ROYAL STUARTS OR A BRANCH OF THE FAMILY SINCE 1371; PARTS OF IT DATE BACK EVEN FURTHER, TO A 12TH-CENTURY TOWER THAT SERVED AS A HUNTING LODGE.

BONNIE PRINCE CHARLIE. Prince Charles Edward Stuart, was the son of the Old Pretender and raised his father's standard in Scotland to launch the '45 rising. This portrait, by the French painter Maurice Quentin de la Tour, is more robust, if less romantic, than some better-known images of the prince.

Contemporaries judged the Massacre of Glencoe by its genocidal intention, and were appalled by its premeditation and treachery. Its principal author, the Scottish secretary of state Lord Stair, was forced from office, but King William, who had authorized Stair's plan, was shielded from censure. Though never forgotten, the massacre had few immediate consequences, and the Jacobite cause showed no signs of reviving.

During the early 1700s, the hopes of the exiled Stuarts were sustained by the support of Louis XIV of France, who was at war with Britain. Encouraged by reports of Scottish discontents following the union with England, a small French fleet reached the Firth of Forth carrying the Old Pretender, only to be chased away by a powerful British naval demonstration. The Highlands remained quiet until September 1715, when the Earl of Mar proclaimed James VIII. The unpopularity of the Union and the new German king gave the enterprise some prospect of success, but time and opportunities were squandered. Mar procrastinated and then fought an indecisive engagement against the Duke of Argyll at Sheriffmuir which checked any further advance; meanwhile a small force, including a few hundred English Jacobites, marched south as far as Preston, only to be surrounded and forced to surrender. By December 1715, when James himself landed at Peterhead, the rising was visibly doomed, and in the following February he sailed back to France.

Four years later, the international situation had changed radically. Now it was Spanish ships that landed a few hundred soldiers and a handful of Jacobites at Kintail as part of a larger invasion plan that was foiled by the weather. Eilean Donan Castle was captured, but most of the clans hung back and a defeat at Glenshiel effectively ended the enterprise.

Another generation passed, and by 1745 Killiecrankie and even the Union and the '15 were becoming dim memories. On any rational calculation the Stuart cause had become utterly hopeless. Yet, paradoxically, this was the year in which it would come closest to success and give rise to the romantic legend of 'Bonnie Prince Charlie'. In July, Prince Charles Edward Stuart, son of the Old Pretender, landed on the west coast with seven followers. On 19 August he raised his standard at Glenfinnan and slowly gathered support from the clans. The government's forces, led by Sir John Cope, marched north but failed to engage the Jacobites and were outmanoeuvred. The prince's Highlanders entered Edinburgh and then, when Cope's tardy pursuit reached Prestonpans, launched a surprise attack on 17 September that decided the battle within a quarter of an hour.

All of Scotland except a handful of government-held castles submitted to the Jacobites, but few Lowlanders took up arms on the prince's behalf. Holyrood Palace in Edinburgh once again held a royal court, while Edinburgh Castle, at the other end of the Royal Mile, defied the prince's forces. Nevertheless, early in November he led them into England and began to march south. Despite a mild panic in London, the prospects of the little army (at its strongest only about 10,000 men) soon began to look gloomy. In Lancashire, a Jacobite stronghold, a single regiment was recruited, but elsewhere there were no enthusiastic welcomes for the invaders. Hopes of French help faded and three Hanoverian armies began to close in. On 5 December the prince's army reached Derby, but at a council of war the decision was taken to turn back.

Such a retreat might have demoralized a regular army. But Highlanders were never completely comfortable when too far from home to slip away if things went wrong, and the prince's following reached Scotland in good order. It was even reinforced and for a time besieged Stirling Castle; and when the first government troops arrived from the south, the Highlanders won a last victory at Falkirk on 17 January 1746. But after that they were increasingly outnumbered and forced to fall back to the north. With his army reduced to 5,000 men, Charles made a final, ill-advised stand on Culloden Moor, where the government artillery took a heavy toll and bullets and bayonets finally broke the much-feared Highland charge. While the victorious troops of 'Butcher' Cumberland took savage reprisals, Charles became a fugitive, protected by the faithful at the risk of their lives; their devotion and the prince's perils ensured that the '45 would be remembered as an episode of high romance. But when Charles finally took ship to France in September 1746, the Jacobite adventure was over for good.

THE JACOBITE HEROINE FLORA MACDONALD BECAME A CELEBRITY AFTER SMUGGLING THE FUGITIVE YOUNG PRETENDER, WHO WAS DRESSED AS A WOMAN, FROM BENBECULA TO SKYE; FLORA'S PORTRAIT WAS PAINTED BY RICHARD WILSON (ABOVE) AND ALLAN RAMSEY, AND DR JOHNSON AND JAMES BOSWELL WERE AMONG THOSE WHO VISITED HER AT HER HOME AT KINGSBURGH.

THE BATTLE OF CULLODEN WAS FOUGHT ON 16 APRIL 1746, IN HOSTILE CONDITIONS THAT FURTHER DISADVANTAGED THE WEARY JACOBITE TROOPS. OUTNUMBERED AND OUTGUNNED ON THE BLEAK MOOR, THE CLANS WERE MOWN DOWN OR IMPALED ON GOVERNMENT BAYONETS. WITHIN HOURS THE BATTLE WAS OVER AND THE YOUNG PRETENDER HAD BECOME A FUGITIVE.

ACT OF UNION

IN RETROSPECT, THE '45 RISING WAS SEEN AS A COLOURFUL AND ROMANTIC EPISODE. YET THE SOBER TRUTH IS THAT IT NEVER COMMANDED THE SUPPORT OF MOST SCOTS AND, LIKE JACOBITISM AS A WHOLE, HAD ONLY A MARGINAL INFLUENCE ON THE COURSE OF SCOTTISH HISTORY.

The future was decided by others – in Parliament and Kirk, and in the peaceful but not always friendly relations between the Scots and their southern neighbours.

Able to make terms with the new king in 1689, the Scots remained independent, albeit with the same king as the English; they also won greater freedom for their parliament and at last secured a religious settlement that satisfied the majority. The Presbyterian Church became the official Church of Scotland, and it was now the turn of the long-persecuted Covenanters to eject and harass the Episcopalians, who in 1690 founded their own separate church. The Presbyterian Kirk, with its uncompromising attitudes, probity and puritanism, became one of the central, defining facts of Scottish life.

Scotland remained a poor country, and by the last years of the 17th century the economy was in crisis. Repeated harvest failures caused acute suffering, and mercantile expansion was inhibited by the fact that English colonial markets were closed to the Scots. Some began to believe that this was too high a price to pay for Scottish independence, especially since Scotland's king was already based in the south and preoccupied with English affairs – notably the French wars in which large numbers of his Scottish soldiers were shedding their blood.

However, since the English were reluctant to share their commercial advantages, the Scots made a bold effort to create their own mercantile empire. In 1698 a chartered company founded a colonial settlement at Darien on the coast of Panama. The venture became a Scottish obsession, attracting the savings of all classes, until about half of the nation's capital was risked on a single chance. Unfortunately the site was swampy and fever-ridden, everything was mismanaged, and no help was to be had from England when the Spanish attacked and finally overran the

The Parliam.t of Scotland reading the Queens Letter

A DRAMA RE-ENACTED ON A PLAYING CARD. THIS IS ONE OF A SET THAT CAN PERHAPS BE SEEN AS EQUATING POLITICS WITH GAMBLING; IT RECORDS THE STEPS BY WHICH THE SCOTS WERE PERSUADED TO ACCEPT UNION WITH ENGLAND. HERE THE QUEEN IS BOTH THE QUEEN OF DIAMONDS AND QUEEN ANNE, SOVEREIGN WHEN THE UNION WAS FORMED.

colony. Hundreds perished and the nation reeled under the financial blow.

The Darien disaster made the prospect of access to English markets even more enticing. It also pointed up the disadvantages of separation for both countries, and also for their sovereign: as king of Scotland, William III was ultimately responsible for a colonial enterprise that he deplored as a king of England who had recognized the Spanish claim to Panama. English minds were further concentrated when William's death in 1701 brought the childless Queen Anne to the throne and raised the spectre of a disputed succession. The Scottish parliament refused to endorse the Act of Settlement, passed to exclude the Stuarts and ensure that England's next sovereign would be a Hanoverian. This raised the possibility that the Scots would opt for the Old Pretender and again become a potential enemy on the northern frontier; it was enough to swing English opinion in favour of a full union that would replace the English and Scottish states with a single Great Britain.

At first it seemed that the two were so far apart that no deal could be struck. But eventually the English realized that the Scots would have to be accepted as equal citizens and allowed to trade on equal terms; and the Scots were induced to negotiate by an English threat to cut off all imports from Scotland. The terms were hammered out and presented to the Scottish parliament, which debated them for three months during 1706–7 while riots and demonstrations shook the country. Despite passionate, clause-by-clause opposition, the Act of Union was passed by a large majority; a good deal of money changed hands, as was customary in the 18th century, but the result would probably have been the same if it had not. In a celebrated phrase, Lord Chancellor Seafield described the demise of an independent Scotland as 'the end of an auld song'.

THE ACT OF UNION BROUGHT TOGETHER TWO PEOPLES WHO HAD SEEMED OBSTINATELY SET ON REMAINING APART. THE ENGLISH WERE RELUCTANT TO SHARE THEIR MARKETS, WHILE THE SCOTS TREASURED THEIR INDEPENDENCE. EVENTUALLY, IN 1707, POLITICAL AND ECONOMIC CONSIDERATIONS CREATED THE UNION, AND THE KINGDOMS OF ENGLAND AND SCOTLAND WERE REPLACED BY GREAT BRITAIN.

THE SCOTTISH ENLIGHTENMENT

THE 1707 ACT OF UNION PROVIDED FOR THE CONTINUED EXISTENCE OF SOME DISTINCTIVE SCOTTISH INSTITUTIONS. PRESBYTERIANISM REMAINED THE ESTABLISHED RELIGION, AND THE LAWS AND LEGAL SYSTEM WERE LEFT INTACT. THE PRIVILEGES OF THE TOWNS AND THE POLITICAL-LEGAL AUTHORITY OF THE HIGHLAND CHIEFS WERE CONFIRMED.

But although Scots were represented in the Houses of Parliament at Westminster, Scottish affairs were now unmistakably determined by a distant and effectively English government.

The early years of the Union were disillusioning. Having ensured that the Hanoverians would succeed to the throne of a united Britain, Parliament had little interest to spare for Scotland. Moreover, some discrimination against Scottish commerce persisted in legislation passed at Westminster, and a poor Scotland found it hard to shoulder the increased taxation introduced to pay for Britain's long war against France. In 1716, when Scots peers proposed to end the Union, the bill was only narrowly defeated.

Matters gradually improved as Scottish merchants began to penetrate formerly closed markets and Scottish landowners introduced more efficient farming methods; as in England, the process was a painful one for many tenants, who were evicted when 'improvers' consolidated holdings into larger units.

Progress accelerated after the middle of the 18th century, and Scotland experienced an extraordinary burst of mercantile, intellectual and cultural activity, out of all proportion to the size, resources and population of the country. The philosophers Hume and Reid, the historians Robertson and Ferguson, the scientists Joseph Black and James Hutton and the anatomists and surgeons John and William Hunter made vital contributions to their disciplines. Adam Smith invented the modern science of economics in *The Wealth of Nations* (1776), which described now-fundamental concepts and demonstrated the advantages of free commercial activity over the older Mercantile system of regulation in the interests of the state. Suddenly there were large numbers of first-class Scottish painters, architects and writers, and early in the 19th century the two most influential journals of the period, the *Edinburgh Review* and *Blackwood's*, were published in Edinburgh. The Scottish capital, despite the absence of politicians, expanded greatly with the development of the well-planned, classical New Town. Glasgow, previously insignificant, grew even faster on the profits of transatlantic trade. Working in England, James Watt became one of the pioneers of the

ONE OF THE GREAT THINKERS OF THE ENLIGHTENMENT, DAVID HUME WAS AN AUDACIOUSLY ORIGINAL PHILOSOPHER AND RELIGIOUS SCEPTIC. ALLAN RAMSAY'S PORTRAIT CAPTURES THE PLACIDITY OF THE OUTWARDLY CONFORMIST HUME, WHO LED A COMFORTABLE LIFE AS A COMPANION TO THE WEALTHY, LIBRARIAN, AND DIPLOMATIST; BUT IT ONLY HINTS AT HIS INTELLECTUAL PASSION AND DARING.

Industrial Revolution by decisively improving steam-engine designs, and three Scottish engineers – John McAdam, Thomas Telford and John Rennie – transformed communications throughout Britain. The boom in road, bridge and canal construction profoundly affected Scottish life, one of its most celebrated manifestations being Telford's Caledonian Canal linking the Moray Firth and Loch Linnhe.

Among other developments in the Highlands was a series of military roads driven through them from the 1720s by General George Wade. These were not improvements from the point of view of most Highlanders, since they were clearly designed to control the clans. Wade's roads failed to prevent or stifle the '45, but the rebellion frightened the authorities so thoroughly that retribution was savage and a determined attempt was made to destroy the Highland way of life. Killings, transportations and confiscations were less important in the long run than the abolition of the chief's traditional authority and the ban on carrying arms and wearing tartan or kilts, which was enforced by relentless scrutiny and the harshest possible penalties. The clans submitted, and their martial traditions were mainly perpetuated in the great Highland regiments raised to serve Britain and the Empire.

These and other developments loosened the bonds between chief and clan. Increasingly drawn to the cosmopolitan 18th-century culture, chiefs abandoned their traditionally paternalistic role and began to exploit their ownership of the clan territories. Tenants were evicted to make way for much more profitable sheep-runs, and in the two generations between 1780 and 1850 the Highlands and Islands ceased to be overpopulated and the glens were emptied. The evictions were sometimes carried out with great brutality, although the bewildered people rarely put up any resistance. Some were resettled in coastal smallholdings – crofts – where they were expected to subsist by supplementing their earnings as fishermen and kelp-gatherers; many others left for the Lowlands to work in the new factories or emigrated to Canada and the Antipodes. Although the impact and extent of these Highland Clearances have been disputed, the bitter sense of betrayal felt by thousands of families is well-documented, adding to the poignancy evoked by the destruction of an ancient way of life.

THE LAST OF THE CLAN. THIS SCENE WAS PAINTED BY THOMAS FAED IN 1865, WHEN THE EVICTIONS THAT CLEARED THE HIGHLANDS AND ISLANDS HAD COME TO AN END. DESPITE ITS SENTIMENTAL EDGE IT CAPTURES THE APATHY AND DESPAIR OF PEOPLE WHO HAVE BEEN DISPOSSESSED CULTURALLY AS WELL AS PHYSICALLY.

MILITARY BRIDGES AND ROADS WERE BUILT IN THE HIGHLANDS BY GENERAL GEORGE WADE, COMMANDER-IN-CHIEF NORTH BRITAIN; THIS ONE IS AT ABERFELDY. WHATEVER THEIR MILITARY EFFECTIVENESS, THESE AND OTHER 18TH-CENTURY IMPROVEMENTS IN COMMUNICATIONS HAD A PROFOUND IMPACT ON THE QUALITY OF SCOTTISH LIFE.

THE INDUSTRIAL AGE

IN 1755 AN INDUSTRIOUS SCOTTISH MINISTER, DR ALEXANDER WEBSTER, SIFTED THE AVAILABLE EVIDENCE AND CONCLUDED THAT THE POPULATION OF HIS COUNTRY NUMBERED ABOUT 1.25 MILLION. BY THE TIME OF THE FIRST BRITISH CENSUS IN 1801, THE FIGURE STOOD AT 1.6 MILLION, AND SIXTY YEARS LATER IT HAD CLIMBED TO OVER THREE MILLION.

LOCH KATRINE BECAME WIDELY KNOWN AFTER BEING USED BY SIR WALTER SCOTT AS THE SETTING OF HIS IMMENSELY POPULAR POEM THE LADY OF THE LAKE (1810). THE INFLUX OF VISITORS TO THE AREA, SOON SO WELL-ESTABLISHED THAT IT BECAME THE SUBJECT OF THIS EARLY 19TH-CENTURY PAINTING, MARKED THE BEGINNING OF TOURISM IN SCOTLAND. MEANWHILE, ONLY A FEW KILOMETRES AWAY, INDUSTRIAL SCOTLAND WAS BEING BORN.

All the more remarkable in that large-scale emigration had become an enduring feature of Scottish life, the increasing number of mouths and hands stimulated demand and provided the workers needed for Scotland's Industrial Revolution. Its basis had been laid by the 18th-century expansion of manufactures and commerce. Wool, linen, jute and cotton boomed. Glasgow's trade in tobacco and sugar declined when the American colonies won their independence, but the Clydeside remained a natural artery on which a great shipbuilding industry grew up, and Glasgow became the city-heart of a western Lowlands labouring mightily to mine coal, make iron and steel and cotton, and achieve an ever-increasing range of engineering feats. As in England, the Industrial Revolution was dynamic, dirty and all-too-indifferent to human suffering. The same abuses occurred – child labour, starvation wages and appalling working and living conditions – and were in time ameliorated by legal and other means, although these (again as in England) could not eliminate cyclical booms and slumps or wipe out poverty. All the same, the Industrial Revolution made Scotland one of the powerhouses of imperial Britain, essential to prosperity in peace and vital when there were major wars to be fought.

Ironically, just when large areas of the Lowlands were being taken over by grimy, if productive, industrial sites and cityscapes, Scotland's romantic history and lovely landscapes began to be widely appreciated. Tourism of the modern kind can be dated back to 1773, when England's loudest-roaring literary lion, Dr Samuel Johnson, was persuaded by James Boswell, his Scottish biographer, to visit the Highlands and the Hebrides. For Johnson and Boswell, places and people associated with the 1745 rebellion had already become imbued with romance, and when the ban on Highland dress was lifted, it began to be adopted – often in fanciful forms – as a symbol of a rapidly mythologized past.

But it was the burgeoning cult of nature and the European success of Sir Walter Scott's poems and novels that decisively changed the image of Scotland; and, appropriately, it was Scott who masterminded the 1822 visit to Scotland of King George IV, who obligingly sported a kilt. Scotland's royal connection became permanent after 1848, when Queen Victoria and Prince Albert bought the Balmoral estate and began to have the present castle put up.

The royal taste for tartan and patronage of the Highland Games helped to identify Scotland in many minds with a half-fictional Highland way of life. At the same time, the wealthy and fashionable in England took their cue from royalty and bought or leased Highland estates for grouse-shooting and other activities that became part of the obligatory social round. Consequently, during the Victorian period romantic Scotland and Scotland the upper-class playground co-existed with the land of poor crofters and strenuous industrial enterprise.

During the 19th and 20th centuries, Scots left their country and began to make their mark in the wider world. Without James Watt, William Murdock and other engineers who made their careers in England, the Industrial Revolution would have taken off far more slowly. Scots became leaders in all the main political parties and were accepted in English society, whether as industrialists, scientists or cultural figures. They also played an extraordinary part in the history of the British Empire, providing many of the regiments that fought its battles and the engineers who built its roads and bridges and kept its ships going. As explorers, missionaries and administrators, Scots worked all over the world. Not the least effective were those who willingly or unwillingly left their native land to settle in the United States, Canada, Australia and New Zealand; they or their descendants played a distinguished part as workers or businessmen or statesmen in the building of their new societies.

EARLY DAYS: JAMES WATT'S WORKSHOP IN GLASGOW. IF BRITAIN BECAME 'THE FIRST GREAT INDUSTRIAL NATION', MUCH OF THE CREDIT MUST GO TO THE SCOTTISH INVENTOR WHO MADE STEAM POWER CHEAP AND EFFICIENT. APPROPRIATELY, THE CENTRAL SCOTTISH LOWLANDS BECAME AN INDUSTRIAL POWERHOUSE, BASED ON TEXTILE MANUFACTURE, COAL AND IRON, AND ENGINEERING.

Scotland itself was far from being free of conflict. For many Scots, the most important event of the 19th century was the split in the established church, afterwards known as the Disruption of 1843, when the breakaway Free Church was founded. There were also rebellions against the dominant economic forces. Long submissive, the Highlanders began to resist continued evictions, and although disturbances on the islands of Skye and Lewis were put down with some severity, in 1886 the government was finally moved to give the crofters security of tenure and other basic rights. The Scottish radical tradition dated back to the 1790s although, as in England, government repression drove it underground for long periods. The majority of Scots supported the Liberal Party as the main agent of 19th-century reforms, but from the late 1890s the industrial working class began to develop organizations of its own.

THE GREAT DEPRESSION, TRIGGERED BY THE
WALL STREET CRASH OF 1929, BLIGHTED MANY LIVES
IN THE EARLY 1930S AND WAS NOT FULLY OVERCOME
UNTIL THE SECOND WORLD WAR CREATED FULL
EMPLOYMENT. THE PHOTOGRAPH SHOWS THE SCOTTISH
CONTINGENT OF A 1932 HUNGER MARCH, ONE OF
MANY PROTESTS AGAINST GOVERNMENT POLICIES.

Trade unions slowly grew stronger and trades
councils began to take on a political role.
James Keir Hardie, an outstanding union
organizer, founded the Scottish Labour Party
and in 1892 became the first Labour MP
elected to Westminster. Scots played leading
roles in the emergence of the Independent
Labour Party, a powerful radical force until
the late 1920s under the leadership of James Maxton, and the Labour
Party led by Ramsey MacDonald, which finally eclipsed it.

Although foreign competition was becoming a serious threat, Scotland's industrial base remained strong into the 20th century. During
the First World War of 1914–18 Clydeside was at the heart of the war
effort on the home front, while a grossly disproportionate number of
Scots servicemen lost their lives in the conflict. The wages of industrial
workers failed to keep up with wartime inflation, and their grievances
contributed to the emergence of the 'Red Clydesiders', avowedly revo-
lutionary socialists such as John Maclean, James Maxton and William
Gallacher, subsequently one of the founders of Britain's Communist
Party. Repeated trials and convictions for sedition made them heroes to
many, and the miseries of the post-war period ensured that revolution-
ary radicalism became a Clydeside tradition.

The 1920s and 1930s brought hard times and high unemployment
to Britain, and many experiences – the 1926 General Strike, the
Depression, Hunger Marches and Means Tests – were common to the
entire British working class. All the same, there is no doubt that the
Scots were among the worst sufferers. Dependence on a few heavy
industries proved disastrous as the demand for ships fell away and iron
and coal production declined. Wages in Scotland had always been low,

and still-harder terms for those who stayed in work, along with cuts in unemployment benefit, aggravated problems such as malnutrition, poor general health, high infant mortality and unhygienic, over-crowded houses.

At the height of the Depression, over a quarter of all Scottish workers were unemployed, despite a still-high rate of emigration. There were signs of improvements during the 1930s, and the building of two famous liners, the *Queen Mary* and *Queen Elizabeth*, brought some life to the shipyards. But full employment only returned after the outbreak of the Second World War. Although heavily blitzed, Clydeside again worked at full capacity to produce ships, aircraft, munitions and the Mulberry Harbours that made possible the 1944 Normandy landings. Meanwhile farmers were encouraged to produce more in order to keep down imports, and other industries also adapted to new and larger roles.

After the war, thanks to the Welfare State and general affluence, social conditions improved dramatically. But heavy industry again went into decline, its relatively gradual character tempting successive governments to believe that help from them might halt or reverse the trend. Attempts at diversification were made, but nuclear power and electronics failed to fill the gap, and an attempt to set up a car industry was not a success. Scotland's obsolescent industries were only part of a larger British problem, accentuated by the narrowness of Scotland's industrial base and her geographical disadvantage vis-à-vis the South. Many Scots also felt that the concentration of political power in distant Westminster meant that their country's concerns had a low priority. The Scottish National Party, committed to achieving independence, enjoyed periodic surges of support, but when devolution was on offer in 1979 too few Scots bothered to cast their votes to validate the majority in favour. In the same year, Margaret Thatcher became prime minister, and during the 1980s her monetary policies cut a further swathe through the manufacturing industries. The best news for Scotland was the exploitation of North Sea oil- and gas-fields, bringing wealth that Nationalists claimed would finance independence.

Any summary of the post-war period in Britain inevitably reads as a series of crises and, mostly, failures. Yet in a sense this is a distortion, for standards of living and general welfare rose for most of the period, albeit more slowly in Scotland than in southern Britain. Cars, television sets and other signs of affluence multiplied, and in the late 20th century, despite all the problems, Scotland was a far from despondent country.

THE QUEEN MARY LEAVING CLYDEBANK IN MARCH 1936. THE ENTHUSIASM OF ONLOOKERS WAS JUSTIFIED, FOR THE COMPLETION OF THE GREAT LINER WAS A BRIGHT MOMENT IN THE GLOOM OF THE DEPRESSION. ECONOMIC CONDITIONS FORCED CUNARD TO SUSPEND WORK IN 1932–4, BUT THE QUEEN MARY BEGAN HER 30-YEAR CAREER IN 1937.

THE LIFE OF THE PEOPLE

ABOVE: Glen More on the Caledonian Canal (right) and the Porteous Mob in full cry

The banner of the Leith shipwrights. Shipbuilding at Leith went back to the 17th century, and the town's history as the port serving Edinburgh stretches back even further. With the decline of shipbuilding Leith fell on hard times, only to be remodelled in the late 1980s and the 1990s as a smart suburb of the capital.

SCOTLAND HAS NEVER BEEN AN EASY LAND
FROM WHICH TO WREST A LIVING – A FACT
THAT HELPS TO EXPLAIN THE SCOTTISH
CHARACTER AND THE GREAT THINGS
ACHIEVED BY SCOTS IN THE WIDER WORLD.

FARMERS AND FISHERFOLK

SCOTLAND'S POPULATION HAS ALWAYS BEEN COMPARA-
TIVELY SMALL, AND FOR MOST OF HER HISTORY THE
REASON HAS BEEN THE LACK OF GOOD FARMING SOIL.
THE MOST FERTILE REGIONS ARE THE CENTRAL LOW-
LANDS (ESPECIALLY THE LOTHIANS) AND THE LOWLAND
AREAS ALONG THE EAST COAST.

The worst farming land is found in the Highlands and islands, a fact
that accounts for the prevalence of stock-rearing and the persistence of
a wild way of life in which hunting and raiding promised rewards at
least as satisfying as cultivating the thin, soggy soil.

Farming methods were primitive over most of medieval Scotland,
offering a bare living in good years and widespread famine when the
harvest failed; as recently as the 1690s, the British climate took a severe
turn for the worse and thousands of Scots perished during the lean
years that followed. Scottish law gave landlords the whip hand over
their tenants, enabling them to benefit by payments in kind, work or
cash. The tenants themselves commonly farmed by the 'runrig' system,
dividing the available arable land into strips on which peas, wheat, barley and oats were rotated. But unlike their English neighbours, the
Scots regularly reallocated the rigs (strips) so that no one family of cul-
tivators was favoured, and much of the necessary work was carried out
on a communal basis.

THE DROVER'S HALT: AN EVOCATION OF A RURAL
SCENE ON THE WEST COAST, WITH THE ISLAND OF
MULL IN THE BACKGROUND. THE DROVER WAS AN
IMPORTANT LINK BETWEEN SUCH REMOTE PLACES AND
THE OUTSIDE WORLD.

In both Highlands and Lowlands, the
main surplus, which could be sold for cash,
consisted of livestock. Cattle were walked to
market, often for long distances, by drovers
along well-beaten paths or 'drove-roads'.

After the Union of 1707, English demand for Scottish beef increased greatly, and until well into the 19th century tens of thousands of cattle were driven from the remotest parts of the country through Highland passes, converging on the market at Crieff, just below the Highland Line. The drover, a free agent acting as a go-between, became a familiar figure, north and south, until the railway made his occupation obsolete.

In Scotland, as in England, an agricultural revolution took place during the 18th century. 'Improvers' planted trees, drained, ditched and hedged land, introduced new crops and techniques, and ultimately began the mechanization of farming. From one of the most backward agricultural economies in Europe, Scotland became one of the most advanced. The process also involved the eviction of many smallholders and the consolidation of the land into large, enclosed units. Despite the misery inflicted on rural populations, there was little resistance and large numbers of Scots drifted to the towns to become part of the new industrial order or else emigrated. For those that remained on the land, however, life was certainly better. From the 19th century, Scottish agriculture shared the fluctuating fortunes of the industry in the United Kingdom as a whole. After the Second World War this meant full mechanization and a shrinking workforce, ending the old rural way of life.

In the Highlands, change was more rapid and drastic. The Clearances paved the way for sheep, and later for sporting estates. Families who did not emigrate were relocated, typically to plots of land that were not large enough to provide even subsistence; their occupants, known as crofters, had to supplement their incomes by activities such as kelp-gathering and fishing, and even so led the most frugal of lives. Although legislation led to greater security and better conditions, the satisfactory development of the Highlands remained a seemingly unsolvable problem throughout the 20th century.

Fishing has been important since earliest times, favoured by Scotland's long, many-harboured coastline and multitude of islands. For most of history it was a perilous occupation, undertaken (in the islands until quite recently) in open boats with sails and oars. Salting and smoking made it possible to preserve fish for consumption when other food was scarce, and also created the basis for an international trade of which Scotland became a part. Despite the great variety of species in the waters around the coast, the industry became especially identified with herring fishing, enthusiastically promoted by 18th-century improvers, who built many entirely new villages, though with mixed results. The industry expanded, operating on an increasingly large scale, and with increasingly efficient technology, down to the 1980s. Then the effects of over-fishing began to be felt, and the inevitable contraction was accompanied by conservation measures and adjustments imposed by European Union regulations. Nevertheless fishing remains a significant Scottish industry.

NEWHAVEN OYSTER WOMAN, CAPTURED BY THE PIONEERING SCOTTISH PHOTOGRAPHERS DAVID OCTAVIUS HILL AND ROBERT ADAMSON. THEY HAD A KEEN EYE FOR CONTEMPORARY SUBJECTS, PRODUCING COLLOTYPES OF FISHERFOLK, SOLDIERS AND CHESS PLAYERS, AS WELL AS PORTRAITS AND VICTORIAN SET-PIECES. THEIR BEST WORK WAS DONE BETWEEN 1843 AND ADAMSON'S DEATH ONLY FIVE YEARS LATER.

BURGHS AND MARKETS

UNTIL THE MIDDLE AGES, SCOTLAND HAD CEREMONIAL CENTRES SUCH AS SCONE, WHERE THE KINGS WERE ENTHRONED, BUT NO TOWNS IN THE MODERN SENSE. THEIR DEVELOPMENT IN THE 11TH AND 12TH CENTURIES REFLECTED THE GENERAL EUROPEAN EXPANSION, AND ALSO OWED MUCH TO THE INFLUX OF TRADERS, CLERKS AND HANGERS-ON ACCOMPANYING THE NORMAN FAMILIES FROM ENGLAND WHO INTRODUCED FEUDALISM TO THE SCOTTISH KINGDOM.

CULROSS IN FIFE IS A SUPERBLY PRESERVED EXAMPLE OF A SCOTTISH BURGH WITH A TOWN PLAN DATING FROM THE 16TH CENTURY. THE BUILDING SHOWN HERE IS A TOWN HOUSE OF 1626, REBUILT WITH A TOWER IN 1783. NOTICE THE STEPS LEADING UP TO THE ENTRANCE ON THE FIRST FLOOR.

The newcomers built castles, and the settlements that grew up under their protection in the lowlands became the nucleus of towns. Many of their inhabitants were English, French or Flemish, and their presence hastened the elimination of the Gaelic tongue, accentuating the contrast between Lowlands and Highlands.

An enthusiastic promoter of feudalism and everything that went with it, King David I granted the most substantial of these settlements a legal status. They became royal burghs (boroughs), each furnished with a charter defining its rights and privileges. The king had a direct interest in their prosperity, since the rents paid by the burghs formed a significant percentage of the royal revenue. Most of the chartered privileges were valuable because they excluded potential competitors, for example permitting the burgh to hold markets and fairs that would draw in country people and make it the commercial centre of the area, and also to monopolize local trade with foreign merchants. Similar burghs were created by ecclesiastical authorities and secular lords.

As manufactures and trade developed, burghs on the east coast were particularly active, exporting hides, wool and herring, notably to the Baltic. But the scale of such operations was very small. At the end of the 14th century Scotland's most prosperous burgh, Berwick (ultimately lost to England), had just over a thousand inhabitants, and the forty-eight royal and other burghs boasted an average population of about 600.

Consequently the layout of a burgh was simple: it was essentially a long main street, or High Gate, with a series of wynds (narrow lanes) leading off from each side of it; behind the houses on the main street were plots of land, cultivated by the residents until population pressure in later centuries caused them to be replaced by closes built on to the wynds. This basic arrangement is still visible at (among other places) the Old Town of Edinburgh and at Haddington and Culross. At the main port (gate) of the burgh stood the tolbooth, at which a keeper levied a charge on any produce brought into the town; it eventually became a multi-purpose municipal building, used as the council house and the town gaol. Halfway up the High Gate, the road widened to accommodate the parish kirk, the houses of the wealthiest burgesses, and the temporary stalls put up once a week on market day around the mercat (market) cross. Market trading was closely regulated (in theory, at least), and all goods had to be weighed at the public weighing beam, or tron. The area round the mercat cross was effectively the town centre, where people idled, jeered at malefactors in the stocks, listened to preachers, or, when feeling particularly incensed, rioted. Despite the small size of the burghs, people were huddled together, and even wealthy merchants lived over their shops with their journeymen and apprentices.

Towns grew during the 16th and 17th centuries, but the effects of wars and pestilence prevented growth from reaching proportions that would have changed their character; by 1700 Edinburgh had about 30,000 inhabitants, followed by Glasgow, Aberdeen and Dundee with roughly 10,000 each. During the 18th century, Edinburgh became the centre of a sophisticated society with wide industrial, commercial and intellectual interests, although the city's elite continued to live in tenements along the Royal Mile until the building of the Georgian New Town accommodated them more elegantly and greatly extended the urban area. Glasgow grew significantly, but more slowly, until the Industrial Revolution began the transformation of the Scottish town and landscape.

THE TOWN FAIR WAS A MEETING-PLACE AS WELL AS A SOURCE OF INCOME FOR THE COUNTRY PEOPLE WHO LIVED IN THE AREA AROUND IT, AND IT ALSO BROUGHT NEWS AND IDEAS INTO THE COMMUNITY FROM OUTSIDE. THE LIVELY ATMOSPHERE IS NICELY CAPTURED IN PITLESSIE FAIR (1804) BY THE GENRE PAINTER SIR DAVID WILKIE.

VIOLENT TIMES

AMONG THE MOST STRIKING FEATURES OF THE SCOTTISH LANDSCAPE ARE ITS WEALTH OF RUINS, CASTLES AND TOWERS. MOST OF THESE WERE THE RESULT OF AN ENDEMIC VIOLENCE THAT MADE LIFE PAINFULLY INSECURE RIGHT DOWN TO THE MID-18TH CENTURY.

SMAILHOLM TOWER IN ROXBURGHSHIRE IS A GRIMLY BEAUTIFUL PLACE ON CERTAIN DAYS, BUT ALWAYS EVOKES THE BLEAKNESS AND VIOLENCE OF LIFE IN THE BORDER COUNTRY IN FORMER TIMES. ITS STURDY WALLS, SMALL WINDOWS AND COMMANDING POSITION ON A ROCK SHOW THAT DEFENCE, NOT DOMESTIC CONVENIENCE, WAS THE MAIN PRIORITY OF ITS BUILDERS.

Apart from warring on their English neighbours, the Scots were a turbulent people at home, constantly at odds with one another. The border country was the most unquiet of all. From at least the time of Robert Bruce, Scottish-English hostility encouraged the emergence of 'bonnet lairds' or reivers, tough freebooters whose cattle-raiding was not restricted to peacetime and not always confined to the 'enemy' side of the 'debateable lands'. In southern Scotland, as in the north of England, sudden violence was the rule rather than the exception, as witnessed by the large number of tower houses being built – not castles able to withstand a siege, but humbler places of refuge for people and animals, strong enough to hold out for a while until help came or the raiders rode away. The reivers found patrons among great families such as the Hepburns and the Douglases, and much of the fighting on a larger scale was motivated by family feuds rather than national antagonisms. The conflict between the Black Douglases and the great northern family of Percy was full of epic moments such as the battle of Otterburn, or Chevy Chase (1388), at which the mortally wounded Earl of Douglas was said to have ordered that his corpse should be concealed until victory was assured, when Percy was forced to surrender to it.

Border ballads celebrated triumphs such as Chevy Chase and generally presented the reivers in a sympathetic light. The best-known ballad hero was Johnnie Armstrong, who roamed lawlessly far and wide until 1529, when he was invited to a conference by James V. Armstrong arrived with an escort of thirty-six men which was immediately surrounded by a much larger royal force, after which Armstrong and his followers were hanged on the spot.

However, similar treacheries in the interests of law and order were not appreciated when they were perpetrated by the English. In 1597, when another Armstrong malefactor, 'Kinmont Willie', was abducted on a truce day, one of the Scottish wardens – appointed as border peacekeepers – organized a celebrated raid that rescued the reiver from Carlisle Castle. The Borders and the Highlands were notoriously lawless regions where the king found it difficult to make himself obeyed. In the Lowlands too, though town-dwellers and farmers might be relatively peaceable, the great lords formed political factions whose differences were more often than not settled by violence and treachery. Robert Bruce himself had been guilty of a sacrilegious murder, and in the 15th century the accession of a series of Stewart child-kings encouraged kidnappings, conspiracies and macabre killings.

Some of the infamous episodes were connected with the rise and fall of the Black Douglas earls, who at times controlled the kingdom during the 14th and 15th centuries. One attempt to limit their power was made in 1440 by the governor of Edinburgh Castle, who invited the young earl and his brother to dine at the castle, served up a black bull's head – symbol of death – and then had the youths beheaded. Twelve years after the 'black dinner', their cousin, the 8th Earl, reunited the Douglas estates and built up a powerful confederacy. Another dinner invitation ensued (this time to Stirling Castle), and when the earl rejected James II's attempts to wean him away from his allies, the enraged king stabbed him to death. Realizing that he had committed himself to a blood feud, James stormed the Black Douglas stronghold, Threave Castle, and broke the family for good. Their illegitimate relations, the Red Douglas earls of Angus, reached the pinnacle of their power in the 1520s, before suffering a similar though less final eclipse.

The pattern of violence remained unchanged in the 16th century, with the murder of Rizzio and Darnley and the blood-feud pursued by James VI against the Ruthven earls of Gowrie; during the mysterious 'Gowrie Conspiracy' of 1600, probably engineered by James, it was the Ruthven brothers who died but were condemned to have their family name consigned to oblivion. After the union of crowns in 1603, the cross-border policing became possible and reiving declined. The king, resident in the south, was spared former perils, and pretexts for violence took on new political and religious forms.

HIGHLANDERS AND LOWLANDERS

THE CONTRAST BETWEEN THE RECKLESS HIGHLANDER AND THE PRUDENT LOWLANDER IS ONE OF THE TRUISMS OF SCOTTISH HISTORY AND LITERATURE, MEMORABLY SET OUT IN ROBERT LOUIS STEVENSON'S CLASSIC NOVEL KIDNAPPED.

Documentary evidence over several centuries confirms that the Scots themselves distinguished between the two national types; yet both are relatively recent in origin. In the 12th century, feudal institutions spread from the south across Lowland Scotland; they created a society in which lairds (lords) great and small held their lands in return for performing military duties for their superiors, while exacting military service from their own tenants and material support from their serfs. Towns grew up around their castles and were chartered as burghs, and the presence of Anglo-Norman warriors, merchants and craftsmen hastened the spread of the English tongue all over the Lowlands.

At about the same time, the Highland clans began to take on their familiar forms. They too were the result of a racial diversity that was integrated with the help of a common language: originally British Campbells, French Frasers and Viking Macleods all became part of a 'Celtic' and Gaelic-speaking culture. The *clann* (meaning 'children') was in theory an extended family, bound to the chief by bonds of kinship; this usually had some basis in fact, but in practice many outside groups and individuals, including outlaws and 'broken men', were incorporated into the clan and came to attribute their origin to a suitably remote common ancestor. In many ways the chief was not very different from a feudal lord, giving large grants of land to tacksmen (tenants-in-chief) who in turn leased it to lesser men. However, the tacksman was usually a close relative of the chief, and the concept of kinship was taken seriously: the chief remained the chief even to clansmen who became tenants outside his lands, and when the call went out to take up arms it was the chief, not their feudal lord, that they followed.

A HIGHLAND CHIEF IN ALL HIS FINERY. SIR MUNGO MURRAY IS DRESSED IN A VERY DIFFERENT FASHION FROM CONTEMPORARY LOWLANDERS. THIS PORTRAIT BY JOHN MICHAEL WRIGHT WAS PAINTED AS EARLY AS THE 1680s, AND CONSTITUTES HARD EVIDENCE THAT POPULAR NOTIONS ABOUT TRADITIONAL HIGHLAND DRESS AND ATTITUDES ARE NOT ENTIRELY BASED ON NOSTALGIA.

As we have seen, Lowlanders were just as inclined to violence as the clansmen, so that the difference between them might seem to have been based more on language and economics (Lowland farmer, Highland pastoralist) than on a taste for fighting. But there was also a special ferocity in Highland warriors that unnerved Lowlanders. Feuds between the clans were pursued with murderous intensity, and the most famous encounters were marked by a reluctance to break off, however crippling the losses sustained by the combatants; on a hot day in 1544, at the 'Battle of the Shirts', four hundred Frasers fought a larger alliance of clans, with both sides stripped to their long shirts, until only four Frasers and eight of their enemies were left. An even more remarkable fight was pre-arranged in 1396 between the Clans Chattan and Kay. An enclosure was set up beside the River Tay and thirty warriors from each clan fought to the death, with King Robert III and his court as spectators. Almost to the death: when only a single Kay clansman was left alive, he climbed out of the enclosure and swam to safety across the river while Clan Chattan was declared the victor.

LOWLANDER AND HIGHLANDER, BOTH ON THE RUN, PAUSE FOR A MOMENT IN THEIR FLIGHT FROM THE REDCOATS; A STILL FROM THE 1971 FILM KIDNAPPED. THE TALE BY ROBERT LOUIS STEVENSON HINGES ON THE UNEASY FRIENDSHIP – AND DIFFERENCES – BETWEEN SOBER YOUNG DAVID BALFOUR AND THE FLAMBOYANT JACOBITE HIGHLANDER ALAN BRECK.

A keen consciousness of the difference between Lowlanders and Highlanders first appears in written records of the late 14th century. Since the writers were Lowlanders, the situation is always presented from their point of view: 'The people of the coast are of domestic and civilized habits, trusty, patient and urbane...The highlanders and people of the islands, on the other hand, are a savage and untamed nation, rude and independent...and exceedingly cruel.' So wrote John of Fordham in 1380, echoed down the centuries by Lowlanders like John Major, the early 16th-century historian, for whom the nation could be divided into the Householding Scots and the Wild Scots of the mountains.

Though it is tempting to see the Highland way of life as doomed, in the Middle Ages it flourished. When Norway ceded the Western Isles to the king of Scotland in 1266, the real gainers were the MacDonalds, who became Lords of the Isles and wielded an effectively independent authority over a wide area. The clans played a leading role in the Wars of Independence, and remained formidable even after the Lordship of the Isles was suppressed in 1493. Campbells gradually eclipsed MacDonalds during the great political and religious struggles of the 17th century, but the traditional Highland way of life only went into decline from the 18th century.

TRANSPORT AND TRAVEL

DESPITE THE SMALL SIZE OF SCOTLAND'S POPULATION, THE LANDSCAPE WAS MODIFIED BY HUMAN ACTIVITY FROM VERY EARLY TIMES. THE FORESTS THAT ONCE COVERED ALMOST THE ENTIRE COUNTRY WERE CLEARED FOR LAND, FUEL AND BUILDING, CENTURY BY CENTURY, UNTIL WHAT REMAINED WAS DEVOURED BY VICTORIAN INDUSTRIAL NEEDS.

CHARLOTTE DUNDAS: AN AQUATINT BY AN UNKNOWN ARTIST SHOWS THE FIRST PRACTICAL STEAM-DRIVEN VESSEL UNDERGOING ITS TRIAL ON THE CLYDE IN 1803. LIKE SO MANY PIONEERS, THE ENGINE'S BUILDER, WILLIAM SYMINGTON, FAILED TO BENEFIT FROM HIS WORK, DYING FORGOTTEN IN 1831; MEANWHILE THE FIRST COMMERCIALLY SUCCESSFUL STEAMSHIPS CAME INTO OPERATION NINE YEARS LATER.

Reforestation in the 20th century has been an equally human-initiated process. But not much more could be done to improve communications between small and scattered communities, and for most of Scotland's history the only roads were those provided by nature – tracks beaten along valleys and over passes.

In these conditions most travelling was done on foot or horseback. Goods were carried by pack pony or, for short distances, on sleds. Surfaces were too uneven (when they were not rained into a sea of mud) for four-wheeled traffic; only kings and lairds, going to war or moving from castle to castle to consume rents paid in kind, could muster the manpower needed to keep wagons on course. Internal travel was so slow and laborious that, where possible, people preferred to go by water; and it was no accident that most of Scotland's larger towns were situated on coasts or riverbanks. By the 18th century a network of roads had come into existence linking the main Lowland towns; although they were poorly made and maintained, travel by coach became one of the amenities in Scotland's great age of enlightenment and improvement. Roads also came to the Highlands, initially to contain the threat posed by the clans. From the 1720s General George Wade and his successors laid down some 1,500 kilometres of military roads which failed to prevent the 1745 rising but facilitated the subjugation of the Highlands after Culloden.

Roads more directly intended for the benefit of the Highlanders themselves were built in the first half of the 19th century by a commission appointed by parliament. The Scot in charge of the project was Thomas Telford, one of the key figures of the 'transport revolution' that was simultaneously taking place all over the United Kingdom. Only part of Telford's work was done in Scotland, but there his roads, bridges, harbours and canals not only opened up the Highlands but also created much of the infrastructure needed for Scotland's Industrial Revolution. Another famous figure in the history of transport, John McAdam, devised an inexpensive method of surfacing roads with stone chips that withstood wear and weather, with remarkable efficiency, until the arrival of the automobile; the importance of such an apparently small improvement for traffic of all kinds can hardly be overstated.

The 18th century's answer to the problem of carrying heavy goods was to build canals. The Scots were not infected by the speculative 'canal mania' that ran through England in the 1780s, but half-a-dozen major works were undertaken, beginning with the Forth-Clyde Canal, which opened in 1790. The most spectacular, though not economically the most successful, was Telford's Caledonian Canal, which took advantage of the fault line of the Great Glen, running north-east to south-west across the Highlands, to create a 29-lock waterway linking the North Sea with the Atlantic.

Thanks to another Scottish canal engineer, James Watt, steam power rapidly replaced water power, and the canals went into a long, slow decline that ended only in the 1980s, when they began to be refurbished as leisure facilities. By the 1840s Scotland had an integrated railway system, and in the 20th century the *Flying Scotsman* became Britain's most famous steam locomotive; appropriately, its designer, Nigel Gresley, was Edinburgh-born. On the water, steamers were particularly important in reducing the isolation of the Western and Northern Isles, a trend accelerated in recent times by air services and computer and television links.

THE FLYING SCOTSMAN LEAVES KING'S CROSS STATION IN LONDON ON 11 MAY 1928, MAKING ITS FIRST NON-STOP RUN TO EDINBURGH. THIS FAMOUS LOCOMOTIVE WAS DESIGNED BY EDINBURGH-BORN NIGEL GRESLEY. THE HIGH POINT OF HIS THIRTY-YEAR CAREER CAME IN 1938, WHEN HIS MALLARD BROKE THE WORLD STEAM TRACTION RECORD.

NATIONAL INSTITUTIONS

THE 1707 ACT OF UNION REMOVED POLITICAL POWER FROM SCOTLAND TO THE PARLIAMENT IN LONDON, BUT ITS PROVISIONS STIPULATED THAT A NUMBER OF SCOTTISH INSTITUTIONS WERE TO BE LEFT UNTOUCHED. AMONG THEM WAS THE SCOTTISH LEGAL SYSTEM – ALTHOUGH SCOTS WERE TO DISCOVER THAT THIS DID NOT PREVENT THE HOUSE OF LORDS AT WESTMINSTER FROM BECOMING THE ULTIMATE COURT OF APPEAL FOR THEIR COUNTRY.

THE TRIAL OF MADELEINE SMITH IN 1857 WAS THE SENSATION OF EDINBURGH. WHEN A CLERK DIED OF ARSENIC POISONING, IT CAME TO LIGHT THAT HE HAD HAD AN AFFAIR WITH SMITH, A YOUNG WOMAN OF VERY GOOD FAMILY. THE MAIN EVIDENCE AGAINST HER WAS THAT SHE WAS KNOWN TO HAVE PURCHASED SOME ARSENIC. THE JURY RETURNED THE UNIQUELY SCOTTISH VERDICT, NOT PROVEN.

Some differences between the English and Scottish systems were little more than a matter of terminology: Scotland's advocates and law agents fulfilled much the same functions as English barristers and solicitors. But in important respects Scottish courts and Scottish law were closer to their continental equivalents, and there was a stronger tradition of helping poor people to seek justice through the courts. Centuries of legislation by Westminster, and European Union regulations from the 1970s, eroded many distinctively Scottish elements, but important areas such as the organization of the courts and the interpretation of equity remain separate. The most celebrated survival is the 'not proven' verdict in criminal cases, popularly viewed as expressing greater scepticism than the absolving 'not guilty'. Scottish law has also affected the nature of property ownership and the practicalities of house purchase.

A deeper and wider influence was exerted by 'the Kirk' or Presbyterian Church of Scotland. With its history of early martyrs and heroically resisting Covenanters, the Kirk had a strong emotional grip on a large part of the nation. From 1690 its position as the established church reinforced its authority, and its rigorous Calvinist theology and Presbyterian system of courts meant that the lives of the congregation were closely scrutinized and supervised; non-attenders and other backsliders could be summoned before the Kirk session and made to perform public penance. Sermons, Bible readings, prayers and hymns were the basic elements of churchgoing; at home, fathers were expected to lead their families and servants in communal prayers; and the Sabbath was given over entirely to religious observance, without any concessions being made to notions of leisure or pleasure.

Although the Kirk was plagued by secessions, the dissidents were more rather than less committed to strict interpretations of the Presbyterian-Calvinist system; indeed, their very existence indicates how seriously religious matters were taken right down to the 19th century,

A RAGGED SCHOOL, SET UP FOR PAUPER CHILDREN. THIS PHOTOGRAPH, TAKEN IN 1850, SHOWS THE REV. THOMAS GUTHRIE GIVING A LESSON TO BOYS AND GIRLS. GUTHRIE, A FREE CHURCH MINISTER, WAS A PIONEER OF THE MOVEMENT, WRITING A PLEA FOR RAGGED SCHOOLS (1847) THAT WAS FAMOUS AND INFLUENTIAL IN ITS DAY.

when the Disruption of 1843 was accomplished with enthusiastic popular participation. As in England, the established church tended to lose touch with the new industrial working class, but it was only in the 20th century that the Kirk lost its central position in Scottish life.

The legacy of the Kirk was, inevitably, mixed. Its intolerant puritanism has been blamed for personality defects and the absence of cultural breadth in Scottish life (it is perhaps significant that the Scottish Enlightenment and the development of Scottish art occurred at a time when the Kirk had temporarily lost much of its vitality). On the other hand, Calvinism impelled believers to live a visibly upright and industrious life, and its encouragement of inward reflection and Bible reading promoted a serious-mindedness that may be said to have predisposed Scots to strenuous achievement.

Believing that even the humblest people should be able to read the Word of God, the Kirk was also responsible for Scotland's long-distinctive educational system. Institutions of higher learning existed from the Middle Ages: Scotland possessed no less than three universities (St Andrews, Glasgow and Aberdeen), to which a fourth, Edinburgh, was added after the Reformation. Moreover the idea of providing a universal, if basic, education appeared as early as 1561, when John Knox and other ministers advocated that every parish should have a free school to teach reading, writing and piety, and every burgh a grammar school for further study. Vetoed at the time, the proposal was given legal force by an Act of 1616, and by the end of the 17th century the Scots had acquired a level of literacy unmatched in England and most of Europe for some two centuries.

MAKERS OF THE DISRUPTION OF 1843: NOT COMPLETED UNTIL TWENTY YEARS LATER, THIS IS A GROUP PORTRAIT OF THE MINISTERS WHO BROKE AWAY FROM THE CHURCH OF SCOTLAND AND FOUNDED THE FREE CHURCH. THE HUGE PAINTING WAS THE WORK OF DAVID OCTAVIUS HILL, BETTER KNOWN FOR HIS FAMOUS PHOTOGRAPHIC PARTNERSHIP WITH ROBERT ADAMSON.

SCOTTISH ENGINEERS

SCOTLAND'S EDUCATIONAL TRADITION AND THE CHALLENGES OF EARLY INDUSTRIALISM COMBINED TO CREATE THE PHENOMENON OF THE SCOTTISH ENGINEER. WHETHER BUILDING ROADS, KEEPING A SHIP GOING OR TEACHING AT A UNIVERSITY, HE (ALWAYS HE UNTIL THE LATE 20TH CENTURY) WAS RECOGNIZABLE AS A RARE TYPE OF INDIVIDUAL, COMBINING INTELLECTUAL ABILITY WITH A FIRM GRASP OF PRACTICALITIES.

APPEARANCES DECEIVE: WHAT MIGHT EASILY BE THE AFTERMATH OF A DISASTER IS IN FACT THE GREAT FORTH RAILWAY BRIDGE UNDER CONSTRUCTION. THE SIZE OF THE BRIDGE WAS DICTATED BY THE NEED TO LEAVE ROOM FOR SHIPPING TO PASS UNDERNEATH. AFTER SEVEN YEARS' WORK THE BRIDGE WAS COMPLETED IN 1890.

The first great Scottish engineer was also the one who had the greatest impact on history. James Watt was born in 1736 at Greenock on the Clyde and by the age of twenty-one had become a skilled instrument-maker working mainly for Glasgow University. There he was befriended by the scientist Joseph Black, who encouraged and financed his experiments. Contrary to legend, Watt did not find inspiration in a boiling kettle or invent the steam engine. Steam engines had been used in the 17th century, and in 1708 Thomas Newcomen devised one that was widely employed for pumping water out of mines. But the Newcomen engine was expensive to run because of the quantities of fuel it consumed. Watt hit upon the solution in 1765 when walking on Glasgow Green: a separate condenser would keep the temperature steady in the main cylinder, minimizing heat loss and so substantially reducing fuel consumption. Lacking the capital to develop his invention, Watt worked for eight years as a surveyor on the early Scottish canals, actually supervising the initial work on the Monkland Canal linking Glasgow with the coalfields.

However, he patented his condenser in 1769, and when a business patron with a share in the patent went bankrupt, it was taken over by the Birmingham manufacturer Matthew Boulton. In 1755 Watt and Boulton formed their famous partnership, and Boulton's Soho works began to produce Watt's engines. The firm prospered, and in the 1780s Watt devised a series of further improvements – rotary motion, the double-acting engine, the pressure gauge – which ensured that the steam engine would turn industrial progress into an industrial revolution.

Boulton and Watt's most gifted employee was Ayrshire-born William Murdock, who joined the firm in 1777 and eventually became one of the partners. With curious short-sightedness Watt and Boulton dissuaded Murdock from developing his design for a 'steam carriage', but in 1792, while representing the firm in Cornwall, he succeeded in lighting his house with coal gas. Before the end of the century gas was illuminating much of the Soho works; by 1805 Glasgow was gas-lit, and within twenty years the major cities of Europe and America had followed suit. The end of dependence on natural light or relatively feeble and expensive fuels revolutionized human existence, literally brightening domestic life, making streets safer, and enabling workshops and factories to operate round the clock by shiftwork.

Other Scots were closely involved with the new steam technology. William Symington and Henry Bell developed its application to shipping, while James Nasmyth invented the steam hammer and anticipated the era of mass-production by making standardized automatic machine tools. The manufacture of iron became cheaper thanks to the hot blast furnace devised by James Neilsen. And as well as McAdam and Telford, Scotland produced two major transport and communications engineers in John Rennie, now remembered mainly for his London Bridge, and Robert Stevenson, creator of the famous Bell Rock Lighthouse and founder of a great lighthouse-building dynasty.

Among the most spectacular feats of the late 19th century were the Tay and Forth railway bridges, designed by Sir William Arrol, who was also responsible for London's Tower Bridge. By this time Scotland had established excellent facilities for technical education, and the Scots engineer had become a familiar figure throughout the Empire and beyond (a Scot, Henry Dyer, became the father of Japanese engineering). The tradition was carried into the late 20th century, surviving the decay of Scotland's heavy engineering industries, and had an assured place in the future – at least as presented by the cult TV series *Star Trek*, in which the functioning of the starship *Enterprise* is still dependent on the skills of 'Scottie', chief engineer Mr Scott.

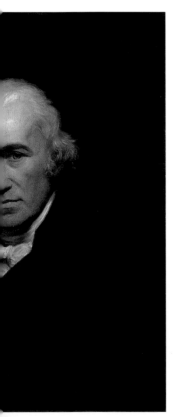

S WATT WAS THE ENGINEERING GENIUS WHOSE IDEAS TURNED TRIAL ADVANCE INTO AN INDUSTRIAL REVOLUTION, DRIVEN BY RST EFFICIENT STEAM ENGINES. ALMOST AS IMPORTANT WAS THE SH ENTREPRENEUR MATTHEW BOULTON, WHO MADE WATT A ER IN HIS SOHO WORKS, DECLARING 'WE SELL HERE WHAT ALL ORLD DESIRES: POWER!'

SCIENTISTS AND INVENTORS

THE FIRST SCOT TO DISPLAY A TALENT FOR PRACTICAL SCIENCE WAS PROBABLY JOHN NAPIER, WHO IN 1614 PUBLISHED DETAILS OF A NEW DISCOVERY: LOGARITHMS. AN ECCENTRICALLY INGENIOUS LAIRD, HE IS ALSO CREDITED WITH INVENTING A FORM OF SLIDE RULE AND THE WORLD'S FIRST MECHANICAL COMPUTING DEVICE: WORKED BY A SYSTEM OF RODS, IT WAS NICKNAMED 'NAPIER'S BONES'.

The first great age of Scottish science formed part of the 18th-century Enlightenment, and most of its outstanding figures belonged to circles close to Adam Smith, David Hume and other intellectual giants domiciled in Edinburgh. The pioneering chemist Joseph Black identified carbon dioxide, thereby proving that the air consisted of more than one gas. He also enunciated the principle of latent heat, which led his protégé James Watt to devise the steam-engine condenser.

Black's contemporaries included John Hunter, the surgeon who initiated the study of comparative anatomy, and James Hutton, author of *Theory of the Earth* (1788). Hutton and his Scottish successors, John Playfair and Charles Lyell, effectively founded scientific geology; in the face of ridicule and charges of atheism, they insisted that the earth's surface had been shaped by pressures, erosion and other forces over many millions of years, and their findings had an impact only surpassed by that of Darwin's *Origin of Species*.

The Industrial Revolution channelled Scottish energies into engineering, but from the mid-19th century major figures appeared in other scientific fields. William Thomson, later Lord Kelvin, was the son of a mathematics professor and became a student at Glasgow University at the astonishingly early age of eleven. He made crucial theoretical contributions to thermodynamics while patenting dozens of inventions which he exploited with commercial shrewdness. He devised significant improvements in electric telegraphy, and in 1866 supervised the laying of the transatlantic cable that linked Europe and North America.

The career of James Clerk Maxwell is less accessible to the non-scientist, but his achievements in the field of electro-dynamics were lavishly praised by Albert Einstein, who declared that without them his own work would have been impossible. Insufficiently appreciated in

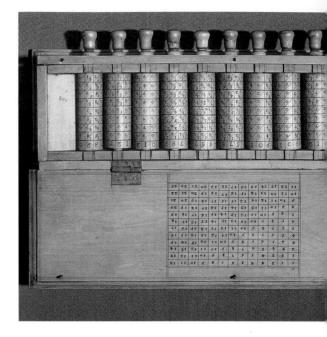

NAPIER'S BONES. THIS WAS THE JESTING NAME GIVEN TO A DEVICE, INVENTED BY JOHN NAPIER OF MERCHISTON, WHICH HAS BEEN DESCRIBED AS THE FIRST COMPUTER. NAPIER'S ONCE WIDELY-READ THEOLOGICAL WRITINGS AND REPUTATION AS A MAGICIAN ARE NOW FORGOTTEN, WHEREAS HIS 'COMPUTER', AND HIS DISCOVERY OF LOGARITHMS, HAVE GIVEN HIM LASTING FAME.

Scotland, Clerk Maxwell spent most of his working life in England, where he set up the well-known Cavendish Laboratory at Cambridge. By contrast, Alexander Graham Bell left Scotland reluctantly at the age of twenty-three, for the sake of his health. In Boston, USA, he taught deaf children while conducting experiments to demonstrate that the human voice could be relayed along a telegraph wire. In June 1875, Bell's assistant Thomas Watson was able to hear a rather banal message transmitted along a wire from another room ('Come here, Mr Watson, I want to see you'), and the telephone was born.

The 20th century was an age of astounding scientific progress, in which huge numbers of researchers and inventors played a part. But two contrasting figures stand out among the many distinguished Scots. Alexander Fleming was a dedicated researcher, spending almost his entire career on the staff of St Mary's Hospital in Paddington, London. Ironically, his world-famous discovery of penicillin was the result of an accident, although it required an acute mind to notice it and draw the appropriate conclusions. In 1928, coming across a slide that had not been cleaned, Fleming saw that the germs on it had been completely destroyed by a mould. Analysing the spore responsible, he discovered that it was a powerful natural antibiotic of the kind he had been searching for since witnessing the results of infections in a military hospital during the First World War. As a result of Fleming's discovery, untold lives were saved.

In the same year, John Logie Baird sent the first moving pictures across the Atlantic. Whereas Fleming was a high-minded researcher who refused to benefit financially from his discovery, Baird led a precarious existence as a professional inventor, making a poor living from products such as his Speedy Cleaner and Baird's Trinidad Jam. Turning to the problem of transmitting moving pictures at a distance, he achieved his first success in 1926. By 1929 the BBC had taken up his invention and begun its first regular service, thereby modestly inaugurating the television age.

JOHN LOGIE BAIRD IN 1925, TINKERING WITH A CONTRAPTION THAT WOULD ENABLE HIM TO SEND A PICTURE TO THE NEXT ROOM. THANKS TO BAIRD, IN 1929 THE BBC TRANSMITTED ITS FIRST TELEVISION PICTURE, AND IN 1936 THE FIRST REGULAR SERVICE BEGAN IN A MEDIUM THAT WOULD QUICKLY CHANGE THE WORLD.

THE WONDERS OF THE TELEPHONE ARE DEMONSTRATED BY ITS INVENTOR, ALEXANDER GRAHAM BELL. IN 1875 BELL SPOKE THE RATHER BANAL WORDS 'COME HERE, MR WATSON, I WANT TO SEE YOU', WHICH WERE RECEIVED IN THE NEXT ROOM, ESTABLISHING THE FEASIBILITY OF A COMMUNICATIONS SYSTEM THAT WAS TO BECOME A GLOBAL NETWORK.

EXILES AND EMIGRANTS

FOR MOST OF HER HISTORY, SCOTLAND HAS OFFERED HER PEOPLE ONLY A POOR LIVING – AND NOT EVEN THAT IN PERIODS OF POPULATION INCREASE OR HARVEST FAILURE. CONSEQUENTLY THE SCOTS HAVE SOUGHT THEIR FORTUNES ABROAD IN MANY ROLES, FROM TEACHERS AND STUDENTS TO WARRIORS AND MERCHANTS.

A trade needing little capital, soldiering became a Scots speciality. Even before the formation of the Auld Alliance, Scots were taking service with the French king. During the Thirty Years War (1618–48), they fought in the armies of France, Germany and Sweden; David Leslie, who led the Scottish army against both Charles I and Cromwell, gained his experience of warfare under the Swedish king Gustavus Adolphus. When Russia emerged as a great power, Patrick Gordon of Ellon, Aberdeenshire, rose to be a lieutenant-general in Peter the Great's army, and Samuel Greig of Inverkeithing reorganized the navy for Catherine the Great and recruited Scots officers.

Scotland's turbulent politics forced many a faction-leader into exile, and Protestants and Catholics alternately sought asylum abroad. With the fall of the Stuarts, many Jacobite adherents chose or fled into exile, providing the manpower of French regiments; and as Scots were simultaneously being recruited into the British army, many 18th-century battles pitted Scot against Scot. The most successful of all the Jacobite exiles was James Keith, who fought for the Stuarts in 1715 and 1719 before joining the Russian service and rising high. Later he became a field marshal in the Prussian army, distinguishing himself in the Seven Years War until 1758, when he was fatally wounded at Hochkirche.

ANDREW CARNEGIE

LIFE

FLINGING MONEY AROUND. THE CARELESS PRODIGALITY IMPLIED BY THIS MAGAZINE COVER WAS NOT REALLY HOW THE SCOTS-BORN US TYCOON ANDREW CARNEGIE BEHAVED. BUT HE DID PART WITH HUGE SUMS TO FUND A RANGE OF WORTHWHILE PROJECTS, AND SCOTLAND AND HIS NATIVE TOWN, DUNFERMLINE, WERE HIGH ON THE LIST OF BENEFICIARIES.

Even during the Middle Ages, Scots merchants were active over much of northern Europe and around the Baltic. Sizeable communities were established in Sweden, Germany and especially Poland, where untapped commercial opportunities offered themselves in the century or so after 1450 when the country was at its most prosperous. Scots seem to have arrived with very limited capital, for versions of the word 'Scot' became current in Poland and Germany to mean 'pedlar'. By the end of the 16th century 30,000 were said to be living in Poland; the figure seems improbably large, but in the early 1600s a member of the Parliament at Westminster warned that, in the event of a closer union with the northern kingdom, England would share the fate of Poland and be 'overrun' by Scots.

In fact the union of crowns in 1603 created opportunities for only a few hundred of James VI's courtiers; even so, the king's liberality was much resented by his new English subjects. However, within a very few

SCOTS IN ACTION. European wars provided Scots with many opportunities to make their way and even make their fortunes. Here Scots and Irish officers take part in a dramatic turn of events in the Thirty Years War (1618-48), arresting the Imperial general Albrecht von Wallenstein on suspicion of treason.

years thousands of Scots were being encouraged to emigrate and settle in Ulster on lands confiscated from the native Irish; the object – to create a Protestant bulwark in a rebellious, overwhelmingly Catholic country – was achieved, with momentous consequences.

The 1707 Act of Union opened up careers in England and the British Empire to Scots, who began to work all over the globe, sometimes settling permanently. London inevitably drew many of the professional class, and the British Parliament at Westminster was of course the only stage for the seriously ambitious politician. From Keir Hardie onwards, Scots were particularly identified with the Labour movement, but the exceptionally large number of Scottish prime ministers has included members of all the main parties: Aberdeen and Rosebery in the 19th century, Balfour, Campbell-Bannerman, Mac-Donald and Douglas-Home in the 20th.

Mass emigration was a rather different phenomenon. Although it was identified with the Highland Clearances it was by no means confined to the Highlands, and went on until the mid-20th century. Scots left for America both before and after the Revolution; John Paul Jones, the first American naval hero, was to raid his native land, just as later the multi-millionaire Andrew Carnegie was to lavish philanthropic dollars on it. Scots settled in many parts of the Empire, but particularly in Canada and above all Nova Scotia ('New Scotland'). Their descendants distinguished themselves in all walks of life, and there are now many more people outside Scotland than in it who identify themselves as Scots, celebrating Hogmanay and holding Highland Games with patriotic fervour.

SCOTLAND IN CALCUTTA. This 1905 menu cover for a St Andrew's Day celebration dinner is crammed with familiar symbols of Scottishness intended to remind the community in India of its roots. Active everywhere in the British Empire, Scots were especially prominent in India, 'the jewel in the Crown', as administrators, soldiers, engineers and missionaries.

MISSIONARIES AND EXPLORERS

AS WELL AS WORKING AND SETTLING ALL OVER THE GLOBE, SCOTS PLAYED A CONSIDERABLE PART IN MAPPING REGIONS PREVIOUSLY UNKNOWN TO EUROPEANS. IN 1789 ALEXANDER MACKENZIE MADE AN EPIC, HUNDRED-DAY JOURNEY ACROSS CANADA'S GREAT SLAVE LAKE AND DOWN THE COUNTRY'S LONGEST RIVER, NOW NAMED AFTER HIM; HOPING TO REACH THE PACIFIC, HE EMERGED INSTEAD ON THE SHORES OF THE ARCTIC OCEAN.

Three years later he achieved his original ambition, becoming the first person to cross North America from shore to shore. Other Scots helped to map both polar regions, but it was Africa that seemed to have the most enduring attraction. As a young man James Bruce appears to have travelled to get over the death of his wife, touring Europe and becoming British Consul in Algiers. Then in 1768, when he was thirty-eight, he travelled in Ethiopia, where he located the source of the Blue Nile, took part in a civil war, and had adventures that were widely disbelieved on his return, though subsequently verified.

Bruce seems to have been driven on by wanderlust, whereas Mungo Park was professionally dedicated to exploration. After serving with distinction as assistant surgeon on an expedition to Sumatra, the twenty-four-year-old Park was chosen to seek the mighty, still-mysterious River Niger in West Africa. Accompanied by a handful of Africans, he was imprisoned for four months by Arabs, suffered terrible privations, but managed to explore the upper reaches of the river.

Returning to Britain in 1797, he became famous after publishing his *Travels in the Interior of Africa*. He settled down in Scotland, but was tempted back in 1805 to lead a far larger but less fortunate expedition. Only a handful survived hostile tribes, fever and dysentery, including Park himself, who remained determined to follow the entire course of the river; he and his companions were drowned while trying to escape a native attack. Another victim of Africa was Alexander Gordon Laing, a military man with a commission from the Colonial Office to find the fabled city of Timbuktu, far in the inte-

THE EXPLORER AT HIS EASE: IN THIS PORTRAIT BY POMPEO BATTONI, JAMES BRUCE IS VERY MUCH THE 18TH-CENTURY GENTLEMAN, BEAUTIFULLY TURNED OUT. HOWEVER HIS FOUR YEARS OF ADVENTURING IN THE SUDAN AND ABYSSINIA (ETHIOPIA) SHOWED THAT THERE WAS SCOTTISH TOUGHNESS AND RESOLVE BEHIND HIS ELEGANT EXTERIOR.

'DOCTOR LIVINGSTONE, I PRESUME.'

rior. In 1826, having married immediately before setting out, he managed to reach the city, half-dead from wounds inflicted by Tuareg tribesmen. He wrote a letter to his wife, announcing his triumph; two years later she learned that he had been attacked and killed just after leaving the city.

The great Victorian age of African exploration involved many Scots including James Grant, who accompanied John Hanning Speke on the expedition of 1860–3 which confirmed that Lake Victoria was the main source of the Nile. But the most famous of all African explorers was David Livingstone, a medical missionary who had begun his working life in a Clydeside cotton mill at the age of ten. He educated himself by studying at night and qualified as a doctor after training by the London Missionary Society. (The Church of Scotland was opposed to African missionary work at this time, although East Africa was later to become a stronghold of Presbyterianism.) Having been frustrated in his wish to work in China, Livingstone arrived at the Cape of Good Hope in 1841 and within a few years had founded a remote mission on the edge of the Kalahari Desert. The earliest of his explorations took him across the Kalahari, followed by a journey to Luanda on the west coast; from there, in September 1854, he began an epic 4,500-kilometre trek across the continent to the Indian Ocean, discovering and naming the Victoria Falls on the way.

Livingstone's later explorations enjoyed a mixed success. But his fame enabled him to campaign effectively against the slave trade, and in 1871, after his whereabouts had been unknown for five years, he was located at Ujiji on Lake Tanganyka by the *New York Herald* reporter Henry Morton Stanley, who greeted him with the words 'Doctor Livingstone, I presume.' Despite his bad health, Livingstone refused to leave, dying in 1873 on a final journey.

The 19th century also produced some intrepid women missionaries and travellers. Aberdeen-born Mary Slessor settled as a missionary at Calabar, Nigeria, in 1876, adopting – and adapting – many local customs to become virtual chief and actual magistrate of the area. And another Scotswoman, Isabella Bishop, travelled in many places considered too dangerous for the supposedly fragile sex, including Morocco, the Rockies and the East. Her life is a fascinating psychological case-history, since she was a semi-invalid whenever she stayed in Britain but was transformed into a vital woman of action as soon as she went on her travels!

CITY AND FACTORY

LIFE AND WORK IN INDUSTRIAL CITIES BECAME PART OF THE SCOTTISH EXPERIENCE DURING THE 18TH CENTURY AND CAME TO DOMINATE IT IN THE 19TH. IN THE COURSE OF A CENTURY OR SO, THE SPECTACULAR GROWTH OF THE TEXTILE INDUSTRIES WAS FOLLOWED BY THE DEVELOPMENT OF IRON MANUFACTURES, COAL MINING AND ENGINEERING, AND THEN BY GIANT SHIP-BUILDING AND STEEL-MANUFACTURING ENTERPRISES.

Some of the human consequences are apparent from demographic changes. Demand for mill and factory workers began to draw the rural population into the towns and encouraged immigration from Ireland. Many clansmen also drifted south, forming Gaelic pockets in the cities. Consequently the Clearances, by driving them from the land, had a double effect: they simultaneously emptied the Highlands and helped to swell the workforce in the industrial belt of the Central Lowlands, dramatically altering the balance of the Scottish population. At the same time the numbers of Scots soared, despite continuing emigration: it rose from 1.6 million in 1801 to 3.06 million in 1861, eventually peaking around the end of the 1930s at about 5 million.

Industrialization made Scotland an economic powerhouse, but the burdens and benefits were distributed in a grotesquely unequal fashion. The early phases of the Industrial Revolution were horribly harsh north and south of the border, subjecting the working class to long hours of exhausting toil in bad conditions and for little return; but in most respects the Scots were even worse off than their English and Welsh counterparts. Wages remained consistently lower right down to the Second World War, and abuses such as child labour and dangerous working conditions took longer to eradicate. Employers justified their treatment of the workforce on the grounds that Scottish industry could only compete with its geographically better-placed rivals by keeping labour costs low; whether or not this was so, the result was that relations between capital and labour became tinged with a bitterness that was fully articulated when trade union organization became effective; and a number of Scotland's later ills have been attributed to the traumas of the industrial age.

However, not all mills were dark and satanic. A remarkably early and successful

THE INTERIOR OF A WEAVER'S COTTAGE DEMONSTRATES THE PLAIN, SOLID COMFORTS EARNED BY HANDLOOM WORKERS IN THEIR HEYDAY. DURING THE EARLY 19TH CENTURY THEY FOUGHT A LOSING BATTLE AGAINST INDUSTRIALIZATION; MOST, UNLESS THEY WERE ABLE TO TURN TO MACHINE-DEFYING WORK SUCH AS MAKING PAISLEY SHAWLS, WERE FORCED OUT OF BUSINESS.

experiment in capitalist philanthropy was undertaken at New Lanark on the Clyde. In 1783 David Dale, a textile merchant, purchased the site and built an industrial village with housing, schools and shops for the workforce; initially a high proportion were orphaned children who were, by the standards of the time, well treated and carefully educated. In 1800 Dale was succeeded by his now more famous son-in-law, the socialist pioneer Robert Owen, who introduced an even more progressive regime. The commercial success of New Lanark suggests that everything that occurred during the industrial age may not have been an inevitable consequence of the iron laws of economics.

BUILDING A LOCOMOTIVE: CLYDESIDERS AT WORK IN 1955. BORN FROM THE CONJUNCTION OF STEAM POWER WITH SCOTTISH COAL AND IRON, LOCOMOTIVE BUILDING WAS UNDER WAY BY THE 1830S AND FLOURISHED IN GLASGOW, KILMARNOCK AND OTHER CENTRES UNTIL THE POST-SECOND WORLD WAR PERIOD; BY THE 1960S THE INDUSTRY HAD VIRTUALLY DISAPPEARED.

Rural industries such as weaving survived well into the 19th century, but the experience of working-class Scots was essentially that of the city. Jerry-building and slums were among the common features of early industrialism, but here, too, Scotland was particularly badly off. In the expanding cities, imposing municipal buildings were raised and pleasant villas graced the suburbs, but the masses were crowded into hastily built tenements which rapidly deteriorated into slums through overcrowding and neglect. A majority of families lived in one or two rooms right down to the First World War, and many were so poor that they nevertheless took in lodgers. The effects of living in such close-packed poverty, though impossible to quantify, must have been significant and long-lasting.

Material conditions did improve over time, though painfully slowly. Despite the new trauma of the Depression and high unemployment during the 1920s and 1930s, real earnings rose, working hours were cut, welfare benefits made it a little easier to survive bad times or bad luck, and subsidized council housing began to make an impact on overcrowding. Yet, on the eve of the Second World War, there was still an enormous amount that needed to be done. Though Scots had developed a distinctive, indomitable urban culture, they remained a people ill-rewarded for their industrial achievements. Paradoxically, after 1945, with their traditional industries in decline, they would find their lives transformed for the better.

NO MEAN CITY

FROM QUIET CATHEDRAL CITY TO BUSY MERCANTILE CENTRE; FROM SOOTY INDUSTRIAL GIANT TO CITY OF CULTURE: IN ITS ALMOST 1,500 YEARS OF EXISTENCE, GLASGOW HAS PRESENTED A VARIETY OF FACES TO THE WORLD.

LATE 18TH-CENTURY GLASGOW, VIEWED FROM THE NORTH-EAST. THE CITY WAS ALREADY COMMERCIALLY IMPORTANT, TRADING IN SUGAR, TOBACCO AND LATER COTTON; BUT AT THIS TIME IT STILL BOASTED A CLEAN, GREEN APPEARANCE, AS YET UNTOUCHED BY INDUSTRIAL GRIME OR THE VICTORIAN REBUILDING THAT DESTROYED MOST OF ITS GEORGIAN HERITAGE.

Situated beside a ford on the north bank of the Clyde, Glasgow became the site of a church erected by its patron saint, Mungo, in the 6th century. Its early history is obscure until the 12th century, when it was given the status of a burgh. From 1196 Glasgow Cathedral was built on the site of St Mungo's church, and in the 15th century it acquired some importance when it became home to Scotland's second university and the seat of a bishopric. Though primarily a centre of learning, the city underwent its share of upheavals during the Reformation and Covenanting eras, rioted against the 1707 Act of Union, and saw Bonnie Prince Charlie march through on his way to England and march back on his way to Culloden.

Meanwhile Glasgow was on the rise as a mercantile city. Modest exports of coal and herring prompted the city fathers to lay out Port Glasgow in the 1690s; only in the 18th century did dredging the Clyde and reclamation of the banks turn Glasgow itself into a port. The Anglo-Scottish Union opened the American colonies to Scottish trade, and Glasgow's western location gave it a distinct advantage. Importing huge quantities of tobacco and sugar created a group of flamboyant 'tobacco lords' and promoted the growth of naval facilities, financial institutions and manufacturing enterprises whose goods filled the ships on their outward journey to east-coast America and the Caribbean.

Wealth from commerce and manufactures enabled Glasgow to expand, and as early as 1727 the English writer and government agent Daniel Defoe described it as, after London, 'the cleanest and beautifulest and best built city in Britain'. By the 1770s it was even wealthier and expanding still faster.

The American War of Independence ruined the tobacco trade, and in the wake of the crisis Glaswegian businessmen founded the world's first Chamber of Commerce (1783); but the local economy proved strong and diversified enough to survive, and the boom in cotton brought renewed prosperity and swelled the population in the city and its environs.In the course of the 19th century, iron, coal, engineering and above all shipbuilding made Glasgow the heart of a great Central Lowlands industrial belt and the self-proclaimed 'second city of the Empire'. Most of the Georgian and earlier buildings disappeared, and in their place the Victorians put up fine municipal and commercial buildings, shopping emporia on Sauchiehall and other streets, and suburban villas for the middle class. The municipal authorities were in many respects progressive, organizing water, electricity and other public utilities, and in 1896 Glasgow's 'second city' status was confirmed when it laid down the only underground railway system outside London.

The dark side of Victorian building was the huge number of tenements that were thrown up in the city and rapidly degenerated into slums. Overcrowding and the problems that accompanied it were even worse in Glasgow than in other urban areas of Scotland, and the scale of the problem, combined with the operation of powerful vested interests, rendered ineffective the authorities' efforts to tackle it. Working-class poverty and industrial pollution created an alternative image of second-city Glasgow as soot-begrimed, drunken and violent; moreover much of the violence was sectarian, intensified as a result of Irish immigration into the city, and most publicly expressed on and off the football playing field during the local derby when 'Protestant' Rangers met 'Catholic' Celtic.

This aspect of Glasgow life inevitably loomed larger during the depressed years between the World Wars when there was mass unemployment and even the great liner *Queen Mary* lay in the shipyard only half-finished for two years. In Glasgow, as in many parts of Britain, the slump of the early 1930s only exacerbated a widespread distress that had existed throughout the previous decade. During this period Glasgow's image was fixed (to the anger of its respectable citizens) by A. MacArthur's novel *No Mean City* (1935), which described the city's life in terms of the rise and fall of a slum-bred 'razor king'.

Rearmament and war brought back jobs and a sense of purpose. Despite bomb damage, Glasgow entered the post-war era with prospects of an industrial renaissance and a heavy social burden. In both areas of concern, the future was to bring a variety of surprises.

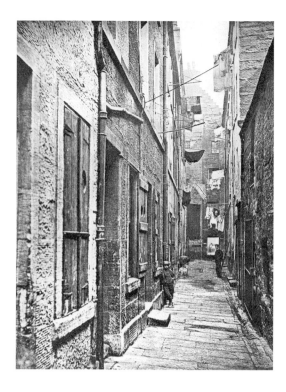

SLUM HOUSING IN THE GLASGOW OF THE 1860S. SQUALID, UNHEALTHY CONDITIONS WERE COMMON IN ALL 19TH-CENTURY BRITISH CITIES, BUT INDUSTRIAL SCOTLAND, AND GLASGOW IN PARTICULAR, SUFFERED FROM SOME OF THE VERY WORST URBAN POVERTY. CONDITIONS WERE AGGRAVATED BY APPALLING OVERCROWDING THAT PERSISTED FAR INTO THE 20TH CENTURY.

GEORGE SQUARE IS, IN EFFECT, THE CIVIC CENTRE OF GLASGOW, WITH A RANGE OF DIGNIFIED VICTORIAN BUILDINGS INCLUDING THE CITY CHAMBERS WITH ITS CUPOLAS (SHOWN IN THE PHOTOGRAPH ABOVE), MERCHANTS' HOUSE AND THE GPO. THESE AND OTHER FAÇADES SURROUND A LARGE OPEN SPACE USED VARIOUSLY FOR CEREMONIES, CELEBRATIONS AND PUBLIC PROTESTS.

TRADITIONAL SCOTLAND

ABOVE: PIPING IN THE HAGGIS AT A BURNS SUPPER (LEFT) AND THE PASS OF GLENCOE FROM LOCHAN NA FOLA

LEITH RACES, AS RECORDED BY THE VICTORIAN PAINTER WILLIAM REED. THE HORSES RACED ON THE SANDS BESIDE THE FORTH, JUST DOWN FROM THE BUSY PORT; THEY WERE WATCHED BY A LARGE CROWD, COMBATIVE AND CELEBRATORY ALIKE, ENJOYING THEIR DAY OUT AND THE STALLS AND ENTERTAINMENTS

KILT, CLAN AND TARTAN; WHISKY AND
PORRIDGE; PIBROCH AND CLAYMORE;
TOSSING THE CABER AND GOLFING AT ST
ANDREWS: SUCH TRADITIONAL IMAGES ARE
SCORNED BY SOME BUT STILL HAVE AN
EXTRAORDINARILY POTENT APPEAL.

THE GAELIC AMBIENCE

NATIONAL IDENTITY IS COMPOUNDED FROM SELECTED HISTORICAL EXPERIENCES, MYTHS AND RITUALS. SUBJECTED TO CLOSE SCRUTINY, MANY OF THESE TURN OUT TO BE NOT QUITE WHAT THEIR UPHOLDERS IMAGINE THEM TO BE, AND THE TRADITIONS TO WHICH NATIONS LOOK BACK ARE OFTEN SAID TO HAVE BEEN 'INVENTED'.

MUSIC AND DANCE AMONG THE GAELS: A SCENE FROM WHISKY GALORE, THE FILM OF COMPTON MACKENZIE'S COMIC NOVEL SET ON THE IMAGINARY HEBRIDEAN ISLAND OF LITTLE TODDAY. ENLIVENED BY RETRIEVING QUANTITIES OF WHISKY FROM A WRECKED SHIP DURING THE SECOND WORLD WAR, THE ISLANDERS ENJOY A CELEBRATION IN THE PUBLIC HOUSE.

There is some truth in the charge; but on the other hand a people are not likely to take on an identity, and believe themselves endowed with certain characteristics, unless these are related to something deep within their natures. However arbitrary the way in which certain stories and customs seem to have taken root, they represent a self-image and a set of implicit values that are certainly authentic.

For two hundred years, the Scottish sense of identity has been closely bound up with the Gaelic past; no rival image of Scottishness, based on urban or industrial life, has had anything like the same acceptance, if only because of its fluidity and impermanence. By contrast, Gaelic culture is now the possession of a tiny minority, and the way of life once characteristic of the Highlands and Islands is safely in the past and therefore unchanging. Scots have proved to be no different from city-dwellers in other 'advanced' cultures in finding attractive such older simplicities as open-handed chiefly hospitality, the kin loyalty of the clansmen, and what look (from a distance) like uncomplicated and independent lives.

Similar feelings are evoked by the ceilidh, the night gatherings in a cottage or croft where neighbours met to sing and dance to the fiddle or pipes, to tell stories from the clan's history or expatiate on the doings of brownies, kelpies and other supernatural beings. Long before the Industrial Revolution, Lowlanders had ceased to see fairies or produce seers with 'the second sight' like Thomas the Rhymer, who was reputed to have spent several years in Fairyland, or the 17th-century Brahan Seer, said to have fallen asleep on an enchanted hillside and awakened in possession of a magic stone with a hole in it through which he could see the future. Sly Scottish humour often casts the possessors of the second sight as victims of their own powers: one was the seer who predicted that a certain man would die within two days; he was proved right when the enraged man slew him and was hanged for it two days later.

To those who ruled Scotland, the clans were not romantic but despised as backward and fulminated against for their lawlessness: when they were not in rebellion they were feuding among themselves or levying black-mail (which originally meant protection-money) on their Lowland neighbours. To James VI they were barbarians who, if it were only possible, richly deserved to be wiped off the face of the earth – a sentiment echoed a century later by Lord Stair, the chief instigator of the Glencoe Massacre. Lowlanders certainly felt no great love for them, and the mainly Highland character of the Jacobite armies helped to ensure that neither Lowland Scots nor English malcontents rallied to the Stuarts during the risings of 1715 and 1745.

Once the military menace of the clans had disappeared, attitudes changed in a remarkably short time. The misty Gaelic past was apparently brought into focus in the 1760s, when James Macpherson published what purported to be translations of works by an ancient epic poet, Ossian. They had an international impact only surpassed by the novels of Sir Walter Scott, which threw a

THE TELLING OF TALES: THE LEGEND, THE BEST-KNOWN PAINTING BY PAUL CHALMERS, WHO WORKED ON IT FOR FOURTEEN YEARS, LEAVING IT STILL UNFINISHED AT HIS DEATH IN 1878. IN THE HIGHLANDS AND ISLANDS, WOMEN PRESERVED THE HISTORY OF FAMILY AND CLAN, PASSING IT ON TO THE NEXT GENERATION THROUGH STORYTELLING.

warm romantic light on the history of Scotland, with a special emphasis on the Highland way of life. Scott's first novel, *Waverley* (1814), was subtitled ''Tis Sixty Years Since'; one of its great themes was the change in men and manners that had taken place in the previous two generations, and its descriptions of Highland dress and customs were couched in consciously nostalgic terms.

Nostalgia and revivalism went hand in hand as Scott's contemporaries among the chiefs began to adopt grandiloquent versions of Highland dress, and the new image of Scotland received the royal seal of approval in 1822 when George IV visited the country and appeared in a kilt. In 1842 Queen Victoria paid her first visit, fell under the spell of the Highlands, purchased the Balmoral estate and built a castle there. Her regular holidays at Balmoral, where she wore a tartan plaid and Prince Albert sported a kilt, served to confirm the quintessential Scottishness of Highland and Gaelic Scotland.

QUEEN VICTORIA AND THE ROYAL FAMILY AT BALMORAL IN 1868. THE QUEEN FELL IN LOVE WITH SCOTLAND ON HER FIRST VISIT IN 1842 WITH HER HUSBAND, PRINCE ALBERT. THEY RENTED, AND THEN IN 1852 BOUGHT, BALMORAL, BUILDING THE CASTLE WHICH BECAME A REGULAR HOLIDAY HOME. THE ROYAL CULT OF SCOTLAND, AND OF THE HIGHLANDS IN PARTICULAR, PROMOTED THE COUNTRY'S GAELIC IMAGE.

CLAN, KILT AND TARTAN

THE GAELIC WORD CLANN CAN BE TRANSLATED AS 'CHILDREN', AND THE NAME-PREFIX 'MAC-' STANDS FOR 'SON OF'. SO THE MACDONALDS (CLAN DONALD) ARE ALL SONS, OR AT ANY RATE DESCENDANTS, OF THE 13TH-CENTURY CHIEF DONALD, WHILE DONALD'S TWO BROTHERS WERE THE FOREBEARS OF CLAN DUGALL AND CLAN RUARI.

So in traditional society each clan could be regarded as an extended family whose members looked to the current chief as their 'father', committed to protect them and entitled to call on them to follow him to war. The kinship basis of clan society explains the existence of Highland customs such as the 'open house' hospitality of the chiefs, the preservation of elaborate genealogies, and the intense loyalties and bitter feuds of the clansmen. 'Highland', here and elsewhere, is shorthand for the Highlands, the Islands and parts of the south-west and border country where the clan system existed until recent times.

Surprisingly, the clans known to history are not of immense antiquity, dating back only to 1150–1350. This has puzzled historians, since there is no obvious reason why clan 'paternity' should have been fixed during that period: Donald and his brothers, for example, were the grandsons of a famous leader, Sommerled, who threw off the Norse yoke and effectively established himself as the first Lord of the Isles; yet it was the brothers, not any of their forebears, who founded clans. A plausible explanation is that the clan system became formalized in reaction to the establishment of feudalism in the Lowlands, which occurred during the late 12th century. Feudalism introduced primogeniture (inheritance by the first-born male) and a legally defined relationship between lord and vassal. Wherever it prevailed, these replaced a social order based on kinship and tanistry. Tanistry involved the election of kings and chiefs from among the male descendants of earlier kings, a procedure suited to a warlike tribal society, since it ensured leadership by an active adult male.

Over the following century or so, laird and clan chief became sharply differentiated, although there was also some degree of mutual influence between the feudal and clan systems. The growth of towns and trade in the Lowlands accentuated the differences, which became the stuff of folk stories and major themes in the works of such authors as Sir Walter Scott and Robert Louis Stevenson.

As was pointed out in an earlier chapter, the clans were not all of Gaelic origin, drawing in British, Scandinavian, French and Flemish groups; the fact that this could have happened indicates that the clan system was particularly well adapted to Highland life.

A HUNTING PARTY: RELIEF PANEL FROM THE TOMB OF ALEXANDER MACLEOD IN ST CLEMENT'S CHURCH, RODEL, ON THE ISLE OF LEWIS. CLAN MACLEOD ORIGINATED IN THE 13TH CENTURY, WHEN THE NORSE PRINCE LIOTR, OR LEOD, INHERITED LEWIS AND HARRIS. BY HIS MARRIAGE HE ALSO ACQUIRED SKYE, WHERE DUNVEGAN BECAME THE CHIEF'S SEAT.

In solchem Habit Gehen die 800 In Stettin angekommen Irrländer oder Irren.

Es ist ein Starckes dauerhafftigs Volck behufft sich mit geringer speiß hatt es nicht brodt so Essen sie Würtzeln, Wans auch die Notturfft erfordert Können sie des Tages Uber die 20 Teutscher meilweges lauffen, haben neben Musgueden Jhre Bogen vnd Köcher vnd lange Messer.

SOLDIERS IN GERMANY: DESPITE THE DESCRIPTION OF THEM AS 'IRISH', THESE WARRIORS ARE MEN OF MACKAY'S REGIMENT, DISEMBARKED AT THE BALTIC PORT OF STETTIN IN 1630, DURING THE THIRTY YEARS WAR (1618–48). THEIR PLAIDS AND RUDIMENTARY KILTS AND BREECHES, THOUGH NOT UNIFORM IN CUT (OR, PROBABLY, PATTERN), MARK THEM OUT AS HIGHLANDERS.

Nor was any clan an exclusively familial grouping, living on its hereditary domains. Clan territories expanded and contracted according to shifts in their fortunes, and some clans migrated from one region of Scotland to another. When a territory was taken over, the 'native men' were usually absorbed into the occupiers' clan, and a similar absorption took place when 'broken men' – sometimes quite large groups of outsiders who had fled from their neighbours' wrath – turned up and were allowed to settle.

The patriarchal character of clan society extended to the ownership of land. All the clan territory was the property of the chief, who leased much of it to tenants-in-chief, who were known as tacksmen; they in turn rented land to tenants who mostly paid in kind or labour. Ownership by the chief, rather than by the community, had little practical significance until the traditional way of life started to come under attack in the late 18th century. Then the clansmen discovered, usually to their bewilderment, that they could be evicted and abandoned to their fate by the more ruthless chiefs; there were other chiefs, of course, who almost bankrupted themselves in their attempt to protect their clansmen, either by keeping uneconomic estates going or backing schemes of resettlement.

In the long run there was no escape from the dispersion of the clans to Lowland factories or lands overseas. To a remarkable degree clan loyalties survived in exile, eventually reinforcing the cult of the Highlands that emerged in the 19th century. Each new devel-

CLAN GATHERING OF MACLEANS ON THE ISLE OF MULL IN 1912: HEADED BY PIPERS, THE CLANSMEN AND WOMEN ARE MARCHING TO THE TRADITIONAL MACLEAN 'CAPITAL', DUART CASTLE, CELEBRATING THE FACT THAT IT HAD BEEN RE-ACQUIRED BY THEIR CHIEF IN THE PREVIOUS YEAR AFTER MORE THAN TWO HUNDRED YEARS IN OTHER HANDS.

A SGIAN DUBH, A KNIFE KEPT IN THE STOCKING. SMALLER THAN A DIRK, IT HAS BECOME AN INDISPENSABLE ELEMENT IN HIGHLAND COSTUME WORN ON FORMAL OCCASIONS; AN EARLIER EXAMPLE OF ITS USE CAN BE SEEN IN SIR HENRY RAEBURN'S PORTRAIT OF THE FLAMBOYANT ALASDAIR MACDONNELL OF GLENGARRY (ABOVE, RIGHT).

MACDONELL OF GLENGARRY, AS PORTRAYED IN 1812 BY HENRY RAEBURN. ALTHOUGH RAEBURN'S STYLE HAD MORE THAN A TOUCH OF THE FLAMBOYANT, MACDONELL'S SELF-CONSCIOUS POSE AS A GRAND HIGHLAND CHIEF WAS CLEARLY A CHOSEN SELF-IMAGE. LITTLE MORE THAN 60 YEARS AFTER CULLODEN, THE HIGHLAND WAY OF LIFE WAS BECOMING A STYLE STATEMENT.

opment encouraged the wearing of Highland dress, and questions of correct tartans and clan affiliations became of absorbing interest.

Scholars have engaged in fierce disputes over the origin and significance of kilts, tartans and other aspects of Highland costume; even the terms used have been denounced by debunkers as non-Gaelic. Since the evidence for the period before 1700 is thin, consisting of a few crude sketches and problematic written descriptions, the issues are never likely to be resolved with certainty. What does seem clear is that Highlanders did wear a form of plaid, a long rectangle of material that could be wrapped round the body and pinned or belted to serve as a cloak. Beneath it, ordinary clansmen were clad only in a long shirt; in battle they tended to throw off their plaids and tie the ends of their shirts together before plunging into the fray. The plaids were covered with stripes or checks which, though certainly the origin of tartans, may not have been uniformly used by a particular clan or exclusively associated with it.

The kilt seems to have developed as a smaller version of the plaid, hanging from the waist to the knee. One claimed originator was an early 18th-century English ironmaster at Invergarry, who persuaded his workers to adopt it so that their upper torsos would be unencumbered during their labours; if so, the kilt must have achieved instant popularity, since it was very widely worn by 1745. So were trews, close-fitting tartan trousers that were worn by the more affluent Highlanders and were adopted by Bonnie Prince Charlie during the '45. Indisputable evidence as to what constituted Highland dress is provided by the Act of 1747 which banned it: tartans, plaids, kilts and trews were proscribed (as were bagpipes) and must therefore already have existed as potent symbols of a martial identity that the British government was determined to destroy.

The ban lasted for thirty-six years, during which time only the regiments raised in the Highlands by the government were allowed to wear tartan or the kilt. The Campbells and other early recruits had already adopted what became known as the government or Black Watch tartan. Later regiments took over tartans associated with the districts in which the clans in question lived, although this does not necessarily mean that such tartans had previously been clan symbols; in fact it is possible that the concept of using setts (tartan designs) as a form of identification originated in the British army.

By the time the ban was lifted in 1782, the Highlands were beginning to seem romantic and a Highland Society had been founded in London; within a few years, chiefs were starting to cut a dash in Edinburgh and have their portraits painted, dressed in a finery that was probably part-invented, by fashionable artists such as Sir Henry Raeburn. The trend was given further impetus by Scott's novels and George IV's appearances in a kilt. Research or imagination attributed setts to all the clans and began a process of name-association and affiliation which would eventually enable almost every Scot to lay claim to a tartan or a clan. Thus, by a strange reversal, the Lowlander succumbed to the Highland image during the very time when the real Highlands were being emptied.

The cult of the Highlands was further elaborated under the patronage of Queen Victoria, when a formal dress code was devised; elements taken from Highland tradition such as the kilt, bonnet, and round sporran (a pouch that hangs from a belt) were combined with a short, close-fitting jacket, decorative silver pistols and a knife thrust into the top of a tartan stocking. A 'cockade' ribbon and eagle feathers, worn on the bonnet, completed the outfit of the Highland gentleman in his 19th- and 20th-century manifestations. Further refinements existed for the most socially ambitious, laid down by the Lord Lyon King of Arms, the supreme arbiter of Scottish heraldry; but at this rarefied level, concerns remote from nationhood are involved.

A FINE GROUP OF 18TH-CENTURY FLINTLOCK PISTOLS, MADE OF ENGRAVED IRON INLAID WITH SILVER. SUCH PISTOLS WERE MUCH SOUGHT-AFTER BY HIGHLANDERS WHO COULD AFFORD THEM; IN WAVERLEY, EVAN DHU'S GOATSKIN PURSE IS 'FLANKED BY THE USUAL DEFENCES, A DIRK AND STEEL-WROUGHT PISTOL', WHILE HE ALSO CARRIES A BROADSWORD AND FOWLING PIECE.

THE WATER OF LIFE

SCOTCH WHISKY IS THE BEST-KNOWN OF THE HIGH-LANDS' GIFTS TO THE WORLD, AND IT HAS BEEN PRAISED TO THE SKIES BY SCOTS OF DIVERSE ORIGINS AND PERSUASIONS. IN GAELIC ITS NAME IS UISGE BEATHA, ' THE WATER OF LIFE' , AND LARGE CLAIMS HAVE BEEN MADE FOR ITS HEALTH-GIVING AND MORALE-BOOSTING PROPERTIES.

A PECK OF MALT. THIS ILLUSTRATION TO THE SONG 'WILLIE BREW'D A PECK O'MAUT' DATES FROM 1840 BUT HARKS BACK TO THE DAYS WHEN ILLICIT DISTILLING WAS A COMMON PASTIME; THE THREE GENTLEMEN SEEM TO HAVE IMBIBED MORE GENEROUSLY THAN THE TITLE SUGGESTS. IN 1840 MALT AND WHISKY WERE STILL SYNONYMOUS.

The poet Robert Burns hailed 'Inspiring, bold John Barleycorn', declaring that 'Wi' usquabae, we'll face the divil!' And the early 19th-century author John Wilson quotes his colleague James Hogg as saying 'If a body could just find oot the exac' proportion and quantity that ought to be drunk every day, and keep to that, I verily trow that he might leeve for ever, without dying at a', and that doctors and kirkyards would go out of fashion.'

Ireland has long had its own whiskey (a deviant spelling also used in the USA), but whether the Scots brought the art of distilling with them from their old homeland, or invented it independently after arriving in the Highlands, has never been determined. For centuries whisky was little known even in Lowland Scotland, although it was gracing the royal table by the late 15th century. It became more familiar with the opening up of the Highlands in the late 18th century, and was soon being promoted by literary men such as Burns and Scott; so that when King George IV made his royal visit to Scotland in 1822, he was well-informed enough to insist upon quaffing Glenlivet with his dinner.

Much 18th-century whisky was produced by illicit stills, mainly to avoid paying the very heavy excise duties in force from 1707; an inevitable result was that a good deal of coarse and impure liquor was sold. The problem was only solved in 1824 (coincidentally or other-wise, following the king's visit) when more reasonable rates were imposed in return for a pledge by the great Scottish landowners to sup-press illegal manufacture and smuggling.

Although the whisky trade had been put on a respectable footing, it was slow to penetrate the English market and remained unknown over-seas. This situation changed with the advent of a new product: blended whisky. Until the mid-19th century, whisky meant malt whisky, which was made entirely from malted barley. The process was long and elabo-rate, involving the soaking, spreading and partial germination of the barley; drying it over a peat fire; grinding and 'mashing', adding yeast, distilling, mixing in spring water, casking the final product and leaving it for at least three years to mature.

In 1826 the new patent-still made it possible to produce a grain (unmalted) whisky much more cheaply and in far greater quantities than the malts. Further improvements followed, including blending in a number of malts with the grain for the sake of consistency and flavour. Requiring little or no maturing, relatively inexpensive and yet of good quality, these blended whiskies became fashionable in England from the 1860s and, with brand names such as Bell's, Dewar's, Haig's and Walker's, became known all over the world.

The success of blended brands angered the malt distillers, who fought a long, losing battle to prevent their rivals from describing their products as whiskies. But in the long run it became clear that the rivalry was largely an illusion, since the two types of liquor served different markets. Most people, including most Scots, bought blended whisky for everyday consumption; but it was widely recognized that malts were the aristocrats, appropriate for special occasions and, in affluent periods, occasions on which the slightest excuse would do. Although there are over a hundred distilleries, every malt has its own distinctive flavour, variously attributed to the quality of the water, the peat used as fuel in drying, and the origin or shape of the cask. The majority of distillers are concentrated on Islay and in the Central Lowlands and the east, but above all in Strathspey, 'the chosen land between the Cairngorms and the Moray Firth', where visitors can follow a 110-kilometre Malt Whisky Trail – if they are lucky enough to find a non-drinker to do the driving.

BOWMORE DISTILLERY, ONE OF SEVERAL PRODUCERS OF FINE MALT WHISKIES ON THE ISLAND OF ISLAY, OFF THE WEST COAST OF SCOTLAND; ISLAY MALTS HAVE A DISTINCTIVELY TANGY FLAVOUR. THE BUILDING IS IN THE TRADITIONAL DISTILLERY STYLE, NOW GIVING WAY IN SOME PLACES TO A MORE MODERN, 'HIGH-TECH' LOOK.

FOOD FOR HEROES

UNTIL THE END OF THE 17TH CENTURY, LAIRDS, TEN-
ANTS AND SERVANTS OFTEN DINED AT THE SAME TABLE,
AND THIS TRADITION OF HOMERIC HOSPITALITY
LASTED EVEN LONGER AMONG THE HIGHLAND CHIEFS
AND THEIR DEPENDANTS.

However, the quality of the fare deteriorated according to the distance of the diner from the laird, with those below the salt having to be
content with 'great platters of porridge, each having a little piece of
sodden meat', according to a 16th-century English visitor.

Porridge was made from oatmeal, Scotland's staple food until the
potato became a serious competitor in the late 18th century. Preju-
diced Englishmen sneered at oats ('A grain, which in England is
generally given to horses, but in Scotland supports the people', in Dr
Johnson's definition), but modern scientific analysis has confirmed that
its high protein content makes it exceptionally nourishing. Which is
just as well, since it provides the main constituent not only for porridge
but for gruels, brose, oatcakes, bannocks, scones and cranachan
(toasted oatmeal, whipped cream and raspberries). Porridge is made by

GREAT CHIEFTAIN 'O THE PUDDING RACE: A HAGGIS IN THE CENTRE OF THE
BOARD, SURROUNDED BY THE INGREDIENTS THAT ARE COOKED IN THE BAG THAT
HOLDS THEM – A SHEEP'S STOMACH. SOME VARIATIONS ARE PERMITTED: HERE THE
CONTENTS ARE ONIONS, ORGANS FROM A SHEEP, OATMEAL, SUET AND PEPPER AND
SALT, PLUS THE TURNIP THAT INEVITABLY ACCOMPANIES THE DISH.

boiling oatmeal in water; it can be consumed with sugar or honey, but the traditional porridge breakfast was salted, served with a glass of milk and eaten standing up or even walking about. A dish of Atholl Brose made an even more back-stiffening start to the day, since it originally consisted of oatmeal stirred into whisky; in these softer days the effect is usually modified by the addition of cream.

Oatmeal is also an important ingredient in various puddings, including the most distinctively Scottish of all dishes: haggis. This is made with the liver, heart and lungs of a sheep, cooked in a bag (the sheep's stomach) along with oatmeal, suet, onions and seasoning. Like many national specialities, it was essentially a way of using up leftovers and pieces of food that were not greatly relished in their own right. The result was a dish which, as *Scotland's Magazine* wryly noted, 'few visitors try twice', but which Robert Burns hailed in his 'Address to a Haggis' as 'Great chieftain o' the pudding race' and credited with responsibility for the warlike ardour of the Scottish soldier. Traditionally eaten with mashed turnips ('bashed neeps'), the haggis has made a comeback as a tourist attraction in refined versions, including at least one that is suitable for vegetarians.

Soups have made a similar transition from leftovers to luxuries, embellished in Scotland by some memorable names. Apart from famous Scotch broth (mutton stock and barley), there are cock-a-leekie (chicken and leeks), partan bree (crab) and (much better than it sounds) cullen skink (smoked haddock). The virtues of Scottish venison and game, Angus Aberdeen steaks, salmon and trout are well known, but the sea has also yielded up a range of delights from Arbroath smokies and finnan haddock (varieties of smoked haddock) to the humble kipper, created from the once-abundant herring.

Scotland produces several cheeses with distinctive flavours, notably crowdie (creamed cottage cheese). But Scots – especially urban Scots – have perhaps been most passionate about pies, pastry, cakes and sweets, which they consume in far greater quantities than their southern neighbours. Among their favourites are the bridie, a semicircular, folded-over meat pasty, and the straight-and-thin-edged Scotch pie. By contrast with the crisp unsweetened oatcake, shortbread originated as a luxury item incorporating fine flour, butter and sugar; one of Scotland's most internationally approved inventions, it was a Christmas and Hogmanay treat, consumed with black bun (a kind of fruit loaf of astonishing density), nuts and whisky.

SPOILED FOR CHOICE. In the past, fishing was a vital part of Scotland's economic life. Fish are still important in the culinary tradition: among the treats pictured are Arbroath smokies (back), baked sea trout (left) and herrings in oatmeal (right). Smoking, originally done to preserve fish, is still valued for its flavour.

SCOTLAND THE BRAVE

THE EARLIEST MILITARY LEADER IN SCOTTISH HISTORY TO BE KNOWN BY NAME IS CALGACUS, A MAN OF OUT-STANDING VALOUR AND NOBILITY ACCORDING TO THE ROMAN HISTORIAN TACITUS. WHEN THE ROMANS LAUNCHED AN ASSAULT ON NORTHERN SCOTLAND BY LAND AND SEA, TENS OF THOUSANDS OF THE CALEDON-IAN NATIVES GATHERED TO RESIST THEM.

The speech said to have been made by Calgacus in AD 84 is oddly reminiscent of the 14th-century Declaration of Arbroath: 'We, who have never been forced to endure the yoke, will fight to preserve our freedom … Let us show, at the very first clash of arms, what manner of men Caledonia possesses.' Although the Caledonians were in fact slaughtered at the ensuing battle of Mons Graupius, the Romans had to give up the attempt to subdue them; and invaders from the south were no more successful for almost 1,600 years.

Little is known of the battles, let alone the political manoeuvres, by which the 5th–9th-century Scots took over the country that was to be named after them. Anglo-Norman military techniques were introduced during the 12th century, and warfare was dominated by mounted and armoured knights, whose tank-like charge could normally be relied on to smash any other type of opposition. By the 14th century this was begin-ning to change, and at Bannockburn the Scots actually benefited from the fact that King Robert commanded too few knights to have any hope of winning a head-on conflict. Instead he chose a superb defensive position in front of the burn (stream), on a slope protected by woods and marshes, and when the English advanced and failed to break the enemy, they found that they had trapped themselves and were cut down. The agents of their defeat were not the few hundred Scottish knights but the thousands of infantrymen, equipped with four-metre-long spears, who deployed in schiltrons, hedgehog-like formations on which their opponents could make no impres-sion.

Bannockburn was the first of several 14th-century battles in which the overweening confidence of lordly chivalry led to disaster. Unfortunately, in the Anglo-Scottish wars the

THE MONYMUSK RELIQUARY IS A BRONZE-AND SILVER-PLATED WOODEN BOX, MADE IN THE SHAPE OF AN ORATORY. IT DATES FROM THE 8TH CENTURY AND WAS BELIEVED TO CONTAIN A RELIC OF ST COLUMBA. IT WAS USED TO BLESS THE SCOTS ARMY, AND WAS CARRIED INTO BATTLE BEFORE BRUCE'S MEN AT BANNOCKBURN.

HIGHLAND SOLDIERS AT MAINZ ON THE RHINE IN 1743, THEIR DRESS AND OCCUPATIONS CAREFULLY RECORDED BY A GERMAN ARTIST. THESE WERE ALREADY IN THE BRITISH SERVICE, TAKING PART IN THE WAR OF THE AUSTRIAN SUCCESSION AGAINST THE FRENCH, TWO YEARS BEFORE OTHER CLANSMEN ROSE IN REBELLION TO JOIN BONNIE PRINCE CHARLIE.

disasters mainly befell the Scots, whom the schiltrons could no longer save once the English realized the role that their own commons could play as longbowmen, breaking up the hedgehog from a distance with showers of arrows, enabling the cavalry to plunge into the gaps with devastating consequences. Like their allies the French, the Scots suffered a series of terrible defeats; unlike the French, they were more often than not reckless invaders, and their smaller resources meant that every disaster, from Halidon Hill (1333) to Flodden (1513) and Pinkie (1547), was a major political, economic and even demographic setback. Perhaps the best that can be said for the Franco-Scottish Auld Alliance is that fighting on two fronts distracted English monarchs enough to prevent them from attempting a permanent conquest of Scotland.

AT CLOSE QUARTERS, 1815: HIGHLANDERS AND SCOTS GREYS GO ON THE OFFENSIVE AGAINST FRENCH CUIRASSIERS AT THE BATTLE OF WATERLOO. A PRIZE OF FIVE HUNDRED POUNDS, OFFERED BY THE DUKE OF WELLINGTON TO THE MAN WHO DISPLAYED THE GREATEST VALOUR IN THE BATTLE, WAS WON BY THE SCOTTISH GENERAL SIR JAMES MACDONNELL.

Meanwhile the Scottish fighting man was becoming a familiar and admired figure on the Continent. The 15th-century attitude towards warfare was a brutally mercenary one, based on dazzling prospects of loot and ransoms which made it better business to take defeated nobles alive than to dispatch them. War-torn France attracted both Scots and English freebooters, and in the early 1420s small armies of Scots, led by the Douglas Earls, fought for the French king. This became a tradition, and Scots royal guards and regiments, their numbers later swollen by Jacobite exiles, served France down to the late 18th century.

However, these were not the only Scots mercenaries. Like other small, poor countries, Scotland eased her population problems and increased her income by sending men abroad to fight for pay – though it should be said that most of these adventurers seem to have chosen masters with sympathetic national and religious affiliations. In 1572, when the Protestant Dutch rose in open revolt against Spain, Scottish companies were raised to assist them and remained involved until Dutch independence was effectively established. During the Thirty Years War (1618–48), Scots enlisted under the banner of the Protes-

tant champion, King Gustavus Adolphus of Sweden, in such numbers that a nervous English council asked the Scots authorities to arrange that departures should take place somewhere closer to home rather than from London! Highlanders also served abroad. Although there is some evidence that mounted Highland warriors existed, most were foot soldiers, for a long time armoured in Norse style and armed with axes and spears; among them were the gallowglasses, islandmen who from the 14th to the 16th century found employment as mercenaries in Ireland.

By the 17th century the Highland warrior known to fame was emerging, armed with a two-handed claymore (broadsword), a targe (leather-covered shield), a dirk (dagger) and pistols; of these, not only the pistols but also the celebrated claymore was a European import, modified to local taste. Few details are known of the clansmen's bloody fights against their Norse overlords or between themselves during the Middle Ages, but it seems likely that they had much the same character as the battles of the Jacobite era, in which the Highlanders stripped off their plaids and charged with a reckless fury that could easily unnerve regular soldiers, especially once the claymores began their bloody work.

The idea that the British state should employ Scots as soldiers was slow to take hold. Recruiting began in the Lowlands under Charles II, although the Royal Scots, still the senior Infantry Regiment of the Line, were originally raised from expatriates in France and only intermittently served the king before beginning continuous service in 1678. The Royal Scots Fusiliers, the Royal Scots Greys and the King's Own Scottish Borderers also date from this period; all fought on the Hanoverian side in at least one of the Jacobite risings – proof, if any were needed, that these were not national rebellions. The poverty of the Highlands made it a potentially rich recruiting ground, but it was only in 1725 that six companies were formed, originally to police the Highlands as an insurance against further Jacobite activity following the collapse of the '15 rising. In 1739 these became the regiment later known as the Black Watch, serving abroad in the War of the Austrian Succession (and, incidentally, leaving the Highlands unpoliced and the way open for the '45).

The battle of Culloden was a microcosm of Scottish military history, since the 'English' army included the Fusiliers and the Borderers, while the Jacobite clans on the other side were supported by a small number of French troops who were actually Scots in the service of Louis XV. Soon after the '45, Britain's European wars and imperial expansion gave an impetus to recruiting in the Highlands, among Jacobite as well as Presbyterian clans; apart from military necessity, employing the clansmen was bound to weaken any remaining antagonism towards the established order.

By the end of the century, such regiments as the Highland Light Infantry, the Seaforths, the Gordons, the Argyll and Sutherland Highlanders and the Queen's Own Cameron Highlanders existed, either in embryo or full-fledged. (All the names used in this paragraph are those under which the regiments became best known; they may not represent the earliest versions or the new forms adopted following the amalgamations imposed in the late 20th century.)

The 18th-century soldier was little better than a slave, and Highlanders did not take easily to inhuman treatment and broken promises; remarkably, no less than sixteen regiments mutinied between 1743 and 1804, only to be broken in hopeless struggles against authority. Nevertheless Scots regiments had already begun their extraordinary feats of arms on behalf of imperial Britain, winning far more battle honours than there is space to describe, from Quebec and Waterloo to the Crimea, the Sudan and South Africa. These were abundantly increased during two 20th-century World Wars, which were also the first mass wars, involving Scots as ready volunteers and conscripts. Their sacrifices and their valour might be described at length but are all present, though unarticulated, in Winston Churchill's remark that 'There is only one thing wrong with the Scots: there are too few of them.'

'LINE UP BOYS!' THIS RECRUITING POSTER WAS ISSUED IN 1915, THE SECOND YEAR OF THE GREAT WAR OF 1914-18. THE JAUNTY IMAGE WAS TYPICAL OF MUCH WAR PROPAGANDA, ALTHOUGH BY THIS TIME CASUALTIES ON ALL SIDES WERE ALREADY HORRIFIC. SCOTTISH COMBATANTS WERE TO SUFFER LOSSES QUITE OUT OF PROPORTION TO THE SIZE OF THE NATION.

HIGHLAND GAMES

ATHLETIC AND MUSICAL COMPETITIONS CALLED 'HIGH-
LAND GAMES' ARE NOWADAYS HELD EVERY SUMMER IN
A VARIETY OF PLACES. DESPITE THEIR PRESENT PEACEABLE
FORM, THEY SEEM TO BE THE REMOTE DESCENDANTS OF
CONTESTS HELD BY HIGHLAND CHIEFS TO PROMOTE,
TEST AND REWARD THE CAPABILITIES OF THE CLAN'S
WARRIORS; AND LEGEND HAS IT THAT THE GAMES WERE
FIRST PATRONIZED BY ROYALTY DURING THE 11TH CEN-
TURY, WHEN THE CONQUEROR OF MACBETH, MALCOLM
III (MALCOLM CANMORE), HELD A GATHERING SOME-
WHERE NEAR BRAEMAR.

Like other Highland traditions, the games had vanished before
1800 and had to be re-invented by enthusiasts, inspired by Sir Walter
Scott, who were beginning to take a romantic view of the Highland
way of life. Revived in the 1820s, the games became immensely popular from the 1840s, when Queen Victoria and Prince Albert bought
Balmoral and spent every autumn there. Ever since then, the royal family has attended the annual Gathering held in September at nearby
Braemar, making it the premier event of its kind.

However, games are being held somewhere in the Highlands during every spring and summer month from chilly April onwards, and the
calendar becomes crowded between July and September. The content
of a gathering varies from place to place, especially since modern show-
manship has reinforced the traditional round of athletics, piping and
dancing with funfairs, mock battles, parachute displays, and the like.
But for most people the heart of the gathering remains a series of contests requiring mighty muscles: throwing the hammer, flinging a
25-kilogram weight over a bar, and above all, because of its uniqueness
to Scotland, tossing the caber. A tree-trunk weighing about 45 kilo-
grams, the caber has to be held upright by the competitor at its base
and flung as far as possible so that it lands end-on and topples forward.
Even more bulk is on view during the tug-'o-war, an event whose
heaving flesh and audible efforts make a nice contrast with the figures
and finesse of the most youthful dance competitors.

Two other traditional sports retain a following. Curling has been
played in Scotland since at least the 16th century. It is a bowls-like
game in which the competitors slide large, round, polished stones
across an ice surface towards a target; its most
distinctive feature is that while the stone is in
motion it is preceded by two sweepers, who
are not clearing a path for it but – depending
on the intensity of their efforts – regulating its
speed and the distance it will travel. Once
played only in the most intensely cold
weather, curling is now an indoor sport.

MAN VERSUS CABER: THE DISPROPORTION
BETWEEN THROWER AND THROWN MAKES IT SEEM
MIRACULOUS THAT THE TOSSING OF THE CABER CAN BE
DONE, LET ALONE DONE WELL. MOST CONTESTANTS IN
THIS AND OTHER HIGHLAND GAMES IN SCOTLAND
ARE NOWADAYS SKILLED PROFESSIONALS, TRAVELLING
THE SUMMER CIRCUIT FROM ONE VENUE TO THE NEXT.

Although participation is confined to northern nations, it has an international appeal and has become a popular feature of the Winter Olympics.

Shinty, a sport mainly played and watched by Highlanders, is even older, figuring in ancient Gaelic legend. Played with a curved stick and leather ball, it bears a general resemblance to hockey and is a close relative of Irish hurling. Still an amateur pursuit, it is fast, furious and not without its dangers.

Fishing and shooting for sport, rather than food, are relatively recent developments. The abundance of salmon, brown trout and sea trout in Scotland's lochs and rivers has long been recognized as a national asset, and conservation measures date back to 14th-century Acts of Parliament. Angling as a pastime was known in the 17th century, but its boom period, and large-scale commercial exploitation, began in the 19th century, when English wealth and the English passion for sport caused southerners to begin a peaceful invasion of Scotland. The same impulse led to the creation of forests for deer-stalking and the turning-over of estates to grouse-shooting and the pursuit of other species of game birds. Here, too, the presence of Queen Victoria and Prince Albert at Balmoral was decisive in encouraging the creation of Highland estates, with new-built fantasy castles and lodges, in which everything was geared to upper-class leisure pursuits. Although there has since been an adaptation to the demands of modern tourism, the situation remains largely unchanged.

CURLING IN FORMER TIMES, ON WINTER ICE. TO JUDGE FROM THIS ENTERTAINING 19TH-CENTURY VIGNETTE, PEOPLE FROM DIFFERENT CLASSES TOOK PART WHEN THE OPPORTUNITY AROSE; THE MOST ARISTOCRATIC-LOOKING PLAYER IS HOLDING THE BROOM BUT SEEMS TO BE MAKING NO EFFORT TO SMOOTH THE WAY FOR THE ONCOMING STONE.

A SHINTY MATCH IN INVERNESS. THE ORIGINS OF SHINTY ARE LOST IN THE MISTS OF GAELIC ANTIQUITY: HURLING AND SHINTY SEEM TO SHARE A COMMON ANCESTRY, DEVELOPING ALONG SLIGHTLY DIFFERENT LINES AFTER THE GAME WAS BROUGHT TO SCOTLAND. THEY ARE STILL CLOSE ENOUGH FOR SCOTTISH-IRISH INTERNATIONALS TO BE STAGED.

SCOTLAND'S OWN

THE GAME OF GOLF IS ONE OF SCOTLAND'S UNDENIABLE GIFTS TO THE WORLD. SOME AUTHORITIES BELIEVE THAT, LONG AGO, A GOLF-LIKE GAME WAS PLAYED ON FROZEN CANALS BY THE DUTCH; BUT IF SO, THERE WAS NO SIGNIFICANT FOLLOW-UP, AND ANY 20TH-CENTURY NETHERLANDER WHO HAS TAKEN UP THE GAME HAS NOT BEEN MOTIVATED BY NATIVE TRADITION BUT BY THE SCOTS EXAMPLE.

GOLF AT ST ANDREWS IN THE 19TH CENTURY: THE SCENE, DOUBTLESS CAREFULLY POSED FOR THE CAMERA, NEVERTHELESS HAS AN ATMOSPHERE COMBINING SERIOUS EFFORT WITH AN AIR OF AMATEURISM NOW RARELY ENCOUNTERED AMONG GOLFERS OF ANY STRENGTH. THE PLAYERS ARE TANTALIZINGLY CLOSE TO THE '19TH HOLE', THE VENERABLE CLUBHOUSE.

Golf may have been played as early as the 12th century at St Andrews, later to be the 'Royal and Ancient' club and law-giver to most of the golfing world. It was played on links – grassy stretches of beach whose sand-dunes created bunkers and other hazards that gave spice to the game. However, the first documented reference came in the form of a prohibition: in 1457, James II and his parliament ordered that 'futeball and golfe be utterly cryed down and not to be used', since such idle pastimes drew men away from practising archery in readiness to fight for their country. But by the 16th century there were royal golfers, and the game was being taken into unexpected regions by enthusiasts such as the monks from St Andrews who continued to play when they were transferred far north to Dornoch in Sutherland; appropriately, Dornoch now has one of Scotland's finest courses. After James VI of Scotland became king of England in 1603, he introduced golf to the southern kingdom, playing with his courtiers at Blackheath, just outside London.

Nevertheless the modern history of golf as a competitive sport begins in Scotland with the first properly organized clubs, founded at Edinburgh (1744), St Andrews (1754) and Musselburgh (1774). Requiring leisure to play and the means to buy purpose-made equipment, golf remained the pastime of a mostly wealthy minority until the later 19th century, when it became more widely popular in Scotland and other parts of the United Kingdom. Changes in equipment manufacture (for example from sewn-leather to rubber-core balls) accelerated the process after 1900, among other things drawing in women competitors. By the affluent late 20th century there was little of the old social exclusiveness left, and golf was played by millions and watched – on the green or on the screen – by millions more.

Other modern sporting activities have followers all over Scotland, and climate and topography are exploited to good effect for internal and external tourism, notably at the winter sports centres in Aviemore and the Cairngorms. Scots also share the world's passion for football, which achieved its modern forms in the country only a few years later than in England. Rugby football is closer to the kind of free-for-all banned in 1457, though played according to strict rules since the 1870s; it has its national stadium at Murrayfield, Edinburgh, which is the Scots venue for the annual Calcutta Cup international against England, contested since 1879, and the Five Nations Championship. Although it generates intense enthusiasm, it does not enjoy the mass support given to Association Football, the world's most popular sport. The Scottish Football Association was founded in 1873, the Scottish Cup competition in the same year, and the League in 1890. Unlike rugby, 'soccer' rapidly became professionalized and acquired a huge following (and a huge number of would-be players) among the working class of the cities. Glasgow's large population was reflected in the overwhelming dominance in Cup and League of the city's teams, Rangers and Celtic, whose 'local derby' encounters were long sharpened by their identification with the Protestant and Catholic sections of the population. Only the Edinburgh teams, Hibernian and Hearts (Heart of Midlothian), and Aberdeen have for brief periods contested the superiority of the Glasgow clubs. In spite of this, hope springs eternal and football thrives all over Scotland.

THE WILL TO WIN: CRAIG BURLEY GIVES HIS ALL FOR SCOTLAND IN THE 1997 WORLD CUP QUALIFIER AGAINST LATVIA AT CELTIC PARK GROUND IN GLASGOW; SCOTLAND WON 2–0. FOOTBALL IS THE SCOTS' FAVOURITE GAME, AND THE NATIONAL TEAM CAN BE CERTAIN OF VOCIFEROUS SUPPORT FROM A LARGE CONTINGENT OF FANS.

LANGUAGE AND LITERATURE

ABOVE: Sir Walter Scott and his literary friends at Abbotsford in a painting by Thomas Faed (left) and Robert Louis Stevenson

John Duns Scotus was the first Scottish writer to become widely known outside his native land. Using the international language of medieval scholarship – Latin – this Franciscan teacher and theologian taught at Oxford and Paris before dying at Cologne in 1308. He was famous for his complex and subtle reasoning.

SCOTS HAVE A LITERATURE TO BE PROUD OF IN TWO LANGUAGES. AMONG THEIR GREATEST WRITERS HAVE BEEN THE NATIONAL POET, ROBERT BURNS, AND TWO WORLD-FAMOUS STORYTELLERS, SIR WALTER SCOTT AND ROBERT LOUIS STEVENSON.

THE GAELIC

THE LINGUISTIC HISTORY OF SCOTLAND HAS BEEN SUR-
PRISINGLY COMPLEX, INVOLVING A NUMBER OF
SPEECH-FORMS WHOSE FORTUNES HAVE FLUCTUATED,
SOMETIMES VIOLENTLY. AT ABOUT THE TIME WHEN THE
ROMANS LEFT BRITAIN, THE BRITONS WHO WERE ESTAB-
LISHED SOUTH OF THE FORTH-CLYDE LINE SPOKE A CELTIC
LANGUAGE AKIN TO WELSH.

A similar vernacular seems to have prevailed among the Picts who
occupied the north, although the evidence about this mysterious people is very sparse; they certainly developed a system of writing, but only
place-names, very late Latin king-lists and symbols carved in stone have
survived to commemorate their separate existence.

Welsh and related Celtic languages belonged to a different group
(called by scholars Brythonic or 'P-Celtic') from the Celtic spoken in

RUNES ON THE WALLS OF THE BURIAL CHAMBER
AT MAES HOWE. THESE GRAFFITI, SCRATCHED BY
VIKINGS IN THE 12TH CENTURY, FOUR MILLENNIA
AFTER THE TOMB WAS RAISED, SERVE AS A REMINDER OF
NORSE INFLUENCE ON SCOTTISH LIFE AND LANGUAGE.
NORN, A SCANDINAVIAN DIALECT, WAS SPOKEN IN THE
NORTHERN ISLES UNTIL ABOUT 1800.

Ireland (Goedelic or 'Q-Celtic'). It was this
language, now known as Gaelic, that was spoken by the Scots who crossed over from
Ulster and, by the 5th century AD, established the kingdom of Dalriada in Argyll. The
activities of Christian missionaries from Ireland helped to spread the use of Gaelic,
directly through their proselytizing and also
by the increased influence that probably accrued to the Scots as the
standard-bearers of an attractive new religion and culture.

The Picts disappeared from history after 843, when they were
united with (or absorbed by) the Scots under Kenneth MacAlpin.

Gaelic became the main national language, although it was never unchallenged, since Norse dialects established themselves in the north and west, and the Teutonic Angles occupied the south-east until the 11th century. Gaelic was probably most widespread at this time, before beginning to retreat in the 12th century as Anglo-Norman influences prevailed at court, and landholding knights, town merchants, craftsmen and monks were imported from the south. Although it may have experienced a temporary resurgence during the turbulent 14th century, the Gaelic-speaking area shrank until it was confined to the Highlands and Islands and part of the far south-west (Galloway), where it flourished until the 18th-century destruction of the clan system and the Clearances that followed.

The most celebrated form of Gaelic literature is bardic verse, composed by professional poets who were attached to the courts of chiefs and passed on their skills and knowledge in schools. The bard's task was to sing the praises of his chief, to inspire the clansmen with ardour on the eve of battle, and to celebrate victories and other happy events. The roots of the bardic tradition lay deep in the Irish past, and linguistic and military links between Gaelic Scotland and Ireland remained close; indeed the two Gaelic languages, though they grew apart, never became mutually incomprehensible. Early in the 13th century a famous Irish poet, Muireadhach, is said to have fled to Scotland, where his descendants, known as MacMhuirichs, succeeded one another as bards right down to the 18th century, mainly in the service of the MacDonalds. Similar bardic family successions were known elsewhere, though not of quite such a long duration.

THE BARD Ossian possessed by poetic frenzy: a romanticized portrait, complete with beard, harp, spear and flaring cloak. Engraved in 1787, it clearly owes more to the largely invented Ossianic epics published by James Macpherson in the 1760s than to the actual poets-in-residence of Highland chiefs.

The 'classical' language used by the bards was not that of the common people, and bardic poems were intricate, ornate and stylized compositions, effectively impossible for the untrained to produce. Patrons became harder to find from the 17th century, as the homeric traditional society of the Highlands began to be affected by outside influences, and the events of the 18th century ensured that both the society and the bards it sustained would disappear; some of the most touching poems of the period are laments for the passing of an entire way of life. However, this was the very period in which Scottish writers and scholars became interested in the Gaelic past and collected examples of its songs and poetry. These also included the separate tradition of popular, non-bardic poetry, which continued into the 19th and even the 20th centuries; among the best-known are work songs, notably the waulking songs sung during the fulling (beating) of textiles. From the 19th century, though often regarded as a quaint survival in an English-language-dominated society, Gaelic was to display a surprising durability.

THE MAKERS

THE LANGUAGE THAT REPLACED GAELIC IN THE LOW-
LANDS WAS A KIND OF NORTHERN ENGLISH THAT WAS
FOUND ON BOTH SIDES OF THE BORDER DURING THE
MIDDLE AGES. THIS EVENTUALLY BECAME KNOWN AS
SCOTS IN ORDER TO DISTINGUISH IT FROM THE SOUTH-
ERN FORM OF THE LANGUAGE, WHICH BECAME THE
STANDARD MODE FOR WRITERS IN ENGLAND ITSELF.

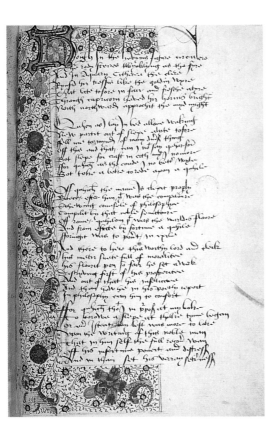

THE KING'S BOOK: A BEAUTIFULLY DECORATED
MANUSCRIPT PAGE FROM THE LONG POEM BY KING
JAMES I. WRITTEN IN ABOUT 1424, SHORTLY AFTER
THE KING'S RELEASE FROM TEN YEARS OF CAPTIVITY IN
ENGLAND, ITS MAIN CHARACTER IS A ROYAL PRISONER,
AND THE NARRATIVE SEEMS TO REFLECT JAMES'S OWN
COURTSHIP AND MARRIAGE.

In the 12th century Scots became the language of the towns, although a form of
Norman French was spoken at court. In Scotland as in England, the vernacular absorbed
the speech of the upper-class minority, but
Norman influence was responsible for the
appearance of continental literary forms such
as the long verse narrative, and therefore
helped to set writing in Scots on a different
path from Gaelic.

However, the first significant writings produced by named Scottish authors were not in
Scots but Latin, the international language of
the Middle Ages. These authors were philoso-
pher-theologians, several of whom achieved a
European reputation; but since there were no
Scottish universities until the beginning of the
15th century, they mainly studied and lec-
tured abroad. During the early years of the
14th century the most famous Scottish
philosopher, Duns Scotus, is recorded as
residing at Oxford, Paris and Cologne. His
writings are still part of the Catholic scholastic
tradition; ironically, because the arguments of
his later followers seemed like absurd hair-
splitting to their Renaissance opponents,
'Duns' was denounced as a fool and passed
into English as 'dunce'.

The first important work in Scots to have
survived is *The Brus* (The Bruce), written in
about 1375 by John Barbour, a scholar who became archdeacon of
Aberdeen and served on two embassies to France. *The Brus* is a
14,000-line narrative of the Wars of Independence, with Robert Bruce
and his faithful follower Sir James Douglas as its heroes. It is a skilfully
written, fast-moving tale which is believed to contain authentic infor-
mation that is to be found nowhere else; but it is also a chivalric
romance that presents the wars as an absolutely just cause and Bruce as
beyond reproach, his feats of arms on the English side discreetly for-

THE THREE ESTATES OF THE REALM ARE TAKEN TO TASK IN SIR DAVID
LYNDSAY'S 16TH-CENTURY MORALITY PLAY, SHOWN HERE IN A PRODUCTION AT THE
EDINBURGH FESTIVAL. THE INCLUSION OF A SCENE AT COURT, AND THE UNSPARING
DENUNCIATION OF THE CHURCH, SUGGEST THAT LINDSAY WAS SECURE IN THE
ROYAL FAVOUR AND IN FACT VOICED THE OPINIONS OF KING JAMES V HIMSELF.

gotten. The poem is written in the short jogging couplets used universally by Scots poets until the 15th century. How effective these could
be is shown by the famous apostrophe to freedom (in modernized
spelling),

> Freedom all solace to man gives:
> He lives at ease that freely lives!

If the surviving material is representative, the struggle against England absorbed Scottish literary as well as military energies: anti-English
sentiments abound in verse chronicles, and even in works such as the
legends of the saints, translated into the Scots vernacular from the standard Latin compilation, *The Golden Legend* (Legenda Aurea). But
England produced a great poet in Geoffrey Chaucer, the author of *The
Canterbury Tales* and *Troilus and Cressida*, and within a few years of his
death in 1400 Scottish writers were responding to his influence by
widening their subject-matter and adopting a variety of verse-forms –
although Scots indignantly repudiate the label 'Scottish Chaucerians',
affixed by English critics to their 15th-century poets.

The first of these was King James I, who became an English captive
at the age of twelve and was only ransomed eighteen years later. Well-
educated by his captors and evidently acquainted with Chaucer and his
successors, James wrote a long poem, *The Kingis Quair* (The King's
Book), in about 1424, shortly after his release. It is an allegory in
Chaucerian style, but with an unusual autobiographical slant: the chief
character is a captive who bemoans his misfortunes until he sees a
beautiful lady walking in the garden below his quarters and falls in love
with her; encounters with Venus, Minerva and other divine beings end
with an assurance that his suit will prove successful. More sophisticated

than any earlier work in Scots, the poem is written in seven-line stanzas of a type used by Chaucer but called, in compliment to James I, rime royal.

The 15th century was a golden age for literature in the Scots language. Towards its end it was summed up in William Dunbar's 'Lament for the Makaris' (Makers, meaning poets or wordsmiths), a roll-call of great dead poets beginning with Chaucer and naming contemporaries such as Robert Henryson and Blind Harry, along with others whose works have mostly been lost; to the roll-call must be added Dunbar himself and Gavin Douglas, who outlived Dunbar. Using a wider range of verse forms and exploiting to the full the colourful diction offered by the vernacular, the Makers excelled in narrative, moral fables, courtly allegories, comedy, and also flyting – contests between poets in which each sought to out-abuse the other.

The Scots were particularly fond of this type of combat, a famous example being *The Flyting of Dunbar and Kennedy*; evidently there were no hard feelings, since Dunbar includes Walter Kennedy among the Makers in his Lament.

Many of these poets were attached to the court, and events such as the disaster at Flodden and the gathering Protestant Reformation had a significant influence on the literature produced during the 16th century. Sir David Lyndsay was a royal herald and a poet whose works of the 1520s and '30s were very much 'state-of-the-nation' pieces, ranging from direct criticism to political advice put in the mouth of a parrot. His anti-clericalism became more open in *The Thrie Estaitis*, a morality play in which Rex Humanitas (King Humanity) is rid of the evil counsellors (vices personified) who surround him. This generalized episode is followed by a scene set in the Scottish court, where John the Common Weal denounces the estates of the realm; the Lords and Commons repent, but the Church remains impenitent and the corrupt and oppressive clergy have to be subjected to summary justice. A rare surviving example of Scots drama, *The Thrie Estaitis* is believed to have been performed at court in 1540; in recent years it has been revived quite often in abridged form, its lawcourt-like procedure proving highly effective both on stage and when played in open-air settings such as Greyfriars' churchyard in Edinburgh.

Late in the 16th century and even afterwards, poets such as

A BOOK OF POEMS BY JAMES VI (JAMES I OF ENGLAND), WRITTEN IN HIS OWN HAND. A PEDANTIC, RATHER CLOWNISH FIGURE, GENERALLY DRESSED IN PADDED CLOTHING BECAUSE HE LIVED IN FEAR OF ASSASSINATION, JAMES WAS A SURPRISINGLY ACCOMPLISHED POET, ALTHOUGH HIS EFFORTS REFLECTED HIS DOGMATIC BELIEF IN HIS OWN GODLIKE AUTHORITY.

Alexander Montgomerie and Sir Robert Ayton continued to write in Scots; and in prose the leading religious reformer John Knox published many violent polemics and a more temperate *History of the Reformation of Religion within the Realm of Scotland* (1586). But by this time the use of Scots as a literary language was in decline. The influence of the Reformation narrowed the range of acceptable subjects, and the 'natural' way in which they could be written about was heavily influenced by the fact that the Scots produced no translations of the Bible, but instead relied on versions in English; Bible-reading became the most frequent and deepest literary experience for most people, with predictable effects on writing (though less so on speech). The trend towards the use of English was strengthened after 1603, when the court removed to London and nobles and courtiers inevitably adapted to the conventions of the southern kingdom; in fact James VI, although himself an author and a patron of writing in Scots, revised the language of his published works to give his English subjects the benefit of his wisdom. Even William Drummond of Hawthornden, a poet who stayed behind in Scotland and lived to 1649, was essentially an English-language writer.

WILLIAM DRUMMOND OF HAWTHORNDEN IS HERE SHOWN LOOKING APPROPRIATELY POETIC. WELL-EDUCATED AND WIDELY TRAVELLED, HE RETURNED TO HIS HAWTHORNDEN ESTATE IN ABOUT 1610 AND DEVOTED HIMSELF TO STUDY AND WRITING, THOUGH HIS LIFETIME (1585-1649) COINCIDED WITH A DRAMATIC PERIOD OF BRITISH HISTORY. HIS BEST WORK IS ELEGIAC IN TONE.

The events of the turbulent 17th century favoured the writing of argumentative and hortatory prose rather than poetry, although few modern readers are tempted by the outpourings of its lawyers and divines. The most original prose writer was the eccentric Sir Thomas Urquhart, now mainly remembered as the translator of Gargantua and Pantagruel (1653), the grotesque epic composed by an equally extravagant and word-drunk French writer, François Rabelais. Urquhart was a royalist who fought and suffered for the cause, dying in exile. The Marquis of Montrose, leader of the royalist campaign in Scotland, was even less fortunate, ending his career on the scaffold – one of the alternative destinies he may be said to have anticipated in his famous lines,

> He either fears his fate too much
> Or his deserts are small,
> That dare not put it to the touch
> To gain or lose it all.

ENLIGHTENED AUTHORS

EIGHTEENTH-CENTURY SCOTLAND PRODUCED A SUPER-
ABUNDANCE OF INTELLECTUAL AND LITERARY TALENT.
THE PHILOSOPHER DAVID HUME ASKED, 'IS IT NOT
STRANGE THAT AT A TIME WHEN WE HAVE LOST OUR
PRINCES, OUR PARLIAMENTS, OUR INDEPENDENT GOV-
ERNMENT, EVEN THE PRESENCE OF OUR CHIEF
NOBILITY...IS IT NOT STRANGE, I SAY, THAT ... WE SHOULD
REALLY BE THE PEOPLE MOST DISTINGUISHED FOR LITER-
ATURE IN EUROPE? '

Edinburgh became known as 'the Athens of the North' even before the building of its Georgian New Town in the late 1760s gave it an appropriate splendour; in fact the cramped tenement-living experienced by rich and poor alike may actually have promoted literary intercourse, encouraging the formation of the clubs and societies that became such a feature of the city. Many leading figures were born in other parts of Scotland and not all of them made their reputations in Edinburgh (Adam Smith was an academic at Glasgow, while Edinburgh-born Hume spent years in England or on the Continent), but a high proportion sooner or later discovered that the capital was the most congenial place in which to settle.

Although Hume and others were conscious of what was being achieved, they had an ambiguous attitude towards their national identity and native tongue. Most of them aimed to write, and some of them to speak, a 'correct' English, purged of all Scotticisms. At the same time, investigation of the past was a major aspect of the Enlightenment, and the end of Scottish independence made an interest in the Makers and 'Old Scots' seem particularly timely. Printed anthologies of Scots verse started to appear in the first decade of the century, and collectors began to record popular ballads and songs, although they were not always able to resist the impulse to 'improve' them by accommodating language and arrangement to the polite standards and regularities of contemporary verse. A few poets wrote in the vernacular and enjoyed considerable popularity; among them were Allan Ramsay, also an important editor-publisher of earlier verse, and Robert Ferguson, who succumbed to religious mania and died in 1774 at the age of twenty-

THE GREAT ECONOMIST: A PASTE MEDALLION OF
ADAM SMITH. HIS BOOK THE WEALTH OF NATIONS
(1776) WAS THE FIRST THOROUGH EXPOSITION OF
PROCESSES SUCH AS DIVISION OF LABOUR
(SPECIALIZATION), OF WHOSE OPERATION IN PIN-
MAKING HE GAVE A CELEBRATED ACCOUNT. THOUGH
BELIEVING IN COMMERCIAL FREEDOM, SMITH ALSO
ADVOCATED A POSITIVE ROLE FOR THE STATE.

THE DREAM OF OSSIAN, by the 19th-century French painter Ingres. This romantic fantasy was one of many pictorial tributes by European artists to the ancient Gaelic poet. Goethe and Napoleon were among the many admirers of Ossian, most of whose works were fabricated by his 'discoverer', James Macpherson.

four. Both were at their best in evoking the gamey side of town life; their work makes a bridge to that of a much greater figure, Robert Burns, at the end of the century. Of the many works written in English prose, two are landmarks in the intellectual history of the world. David Hume's *Enquiry Concerning Human Understanding* (published in its earliest form in 1739) proposed a radical scepticism that is still relevant to philosophical thought. And Adam Smith's *The Wealth of Nations* (1776) provided a fundamental analysis of production and trade on which all later economic thinking has been based.

A figure whose influence was greater than his achievement, James Thomson made a career in London as a dramatist, but is now remembered mainly for *The Seasons* (1730). This substantial, four-part poem was written in the conventionally elaborate 'Augustan' style of 18th-century English verse, but its passionate appreciation of nature was new, anticipating the Romantic movement that would sweep over Europe at the end of the century. The cult of the wild and primitive was given impetus in the 1760s with the publication of poems by a 3rd-century Gaelic bard, Ossian, translated by James Macpherson. Although it later became apparent that Ossian's epics were largely Macpherson's own work, their impact was powerful and long-lasting.

Drama still failed to flourish in Scotland, partly through the hostility of the Presbyterian Church, although it was a minister of the Church, John Home, who achieved the greatest contemporary success (at London's Covent Garden Theatre) with the now-forgotten *Douglas* (1766); during one of the enthusiastically packed performances, a patriotic Scottish member of the audience is said to have bellowed, 'Whaur's your Wully Shakespeare noo?' Scotland did produce its first major novelist in Tobias Smollett, whose *Humphrey Clinker* (1771) glances at Scottish mores and presents events from multiple comic viewpoints. But again a lesser but well-timed work won greater contemporary fame: Henry Mackenzie's *Man of Feeling* swept away the public with excesses of tearful sensitivity. Fortunately, more bracing figures were to emerge, including Robert Burns.

A SCOT'S REVENGE. Lieutenant Obadiah Lismahago, cadaverous, touchy and honourable, is one of Smollett's great comic creations. In this illustration from Humphrey Clinker he has retaliated for being made the butt of a practical joke by luring the prankster, Sir Thomas Bullford, to leap into his own pond.

THE NATIONAL POET

POOR FARMER, POET OF GENIUS AND LUSTY LOVER, ROBERT BURNS HAS BECOME A NATIONAL HERO TO HIS FELLOW-SCOTS. BUT DESPITE HIS CREATIVE ACHIEVEMENTS, HIS LIFE WAS IN MANY RESPECTS A FRUSTRATING STRUGGLE AGAINST HANDICAPS OF CLASS AND ENVIRONMENT; AND IT WAS TRAGICALLY SHORT.

Burns was born on 25 January 1759 at Alloway in Ayrshire, where his father was struggling to earn a living as a tenant farmer. Wide reading made good the deficiencies in Robert's formal education, and by his twenties he was writing good English verse and great Scots poetry. But he was a misfit: earning a meagre living from the soil was demoralizing, and Burns's reputation as a rake and rebel prevented his marriage with the girl he loved, Jean Armour, even though she was pregnant by him and eventually bore him twins.

Burns made up his mind to emigrate to the West Indies, but 'Before leaving my native country for ever, I resolved to publish my poems'. The modest 1786 edition of *Poems, Chiefly in the Scottish Dialect*, though published in Kilmarnock, was so well received in Edinburgh that Burns decided to try his luck in the capital. He received a gratifying reception and was lionized as 'the ploughman poet' by intellectuals and hostesses filled with a dawning Romantic admiration for supposedly uncultivated geniuses. He was able to make some money from a second edition of his poems, and embarked on a number of trips in the Highlands and Borders which later proved to be of use, since they acquainted him at first hand with the Scottish folk-song tradition. He also embarked on a series of amorous adventures while mixing and corresponding with leading figures in Scottish society.

Despite his triumphs, Burns had to return to the plough in order to earn a living. In 1788 he was at last able to marry Jean Armour, and he used the slender profits of poetry to take a farm at Ellisland in Dumfriesshire. He soon became disillusioned with his work ('I have not been so lucky with farming') and began to make ends meet by combining farming with employment as an Exciseman. Then, in 1791, he obtained a full-time post in the Excise at Dumfries. The security it offered was some compensation for the uneasiness Burns felt at becoming an 'estab-

ROBERT BURNS AT THIRTY-FIVE, IN A WATERCOLOUR PORTRAIT PAINTED ON IVORY BY ALEXANDER REID. DESPITE HIS HUMBLE BACKGROUND BURNS WAS FAR FROM BEING THE UNTUTORED GENIUS OF LEGEND; BUT HIS INTEREST IN FOLK MUSIC AND EGALITARIAN SENTIMENTS DID MAKE HIM A NEW VOICE IN SCOTTISH LITERATURE.

[manuscript leaf of 'Tam o' Shanter' in Burns's hand]

lishment' figure, identified with the unpopular task of collecting duties. His still-radical sympathies were clear from poems such as 'Is there, for honest poverty', with its open scorn for 'the tinsel show' of ribbons and rank and its famous assertion that 'A Man's a Man for a' that'. His enthusiasm for the French Revolution came to the attention of the increasingly reactionary authorities, and the threat to his livelihood forced Burns to write and behave with unwelcome discretion.

At Ellisland Burns wrote 'Tam o' Shanter', his comic masterpiece in which the drunken, amorous Tam interrupts a witches' coven and barely escapes with his life. But most of Burns's works of the 1790s were songs, which the poet gathered and furnished with words for two great collections, James Johnson's *Scots Musical Museum* and George Thomson's *Select Collection of Original Scottish Airs*. Though his workload as an Exciseman was heavy, Burns composed the lyrics for hundreds of the folk-songs he had heard on his Scottish travels, humming the tunes and fitting words to them as he went about his duties; among the results were such famous pieces as 'My luve is like a red, red rose', 'Ae fond kiss', 'Comin' through the rye', 'John Anderson my jo' and 'Auld Lang Syne'.

In 1795 Burns's health began to deteriorate rapidly and he died on 21 July 1796; he is now diagnosed as suffering from a heart condition (endocarditis) brought on by rheumatic fever. His exquisite lyrics have endeared him to readers everywhere, but Scots have loved him for his earthy, downright attitudes and sympathy with ordinary men and women. Significantly, he is the only great Scottish writer to be referred to so familiarly (as 'Rabbie Burns'), and the very existence of Burns Night suppers, all over the world where Scots are gathered, bears witness to the lasting impact of his personality.

TAM'S BAD TIMING: A LEAF FROM THE MANUSCRIPT OF BURN'S COMIC POEM 'TAM O'SHANTER', DESCRIBING THE MOMENT WHEN A DRUNKEN TAM MUST LEAVE THE INN AT AYR AND RIDE BACK HOME IN THE MIDDLE OF A STORMY NIGHT. HIS ENCOUNTER WITH WITCHES AT ALLOWAY, BURNS'S OLD HOME, ENDS IN NEAR-DISASTER.

THE BIRTHPLACE. BURNS WAS BORN IN A TWO-ROOMED COTTAGE AT ALLOWAY, NEAR AYR, ON 25 JANUARY 1759. HE WAS THE ELDEST OF SEVEN CHILDREN OF A MARKET GARDENER WHO LEFT ALLOWAY TO FARM AT MOSSGIEL WHEN ROBERT WAS SEVEN. THE COTTAGE STILL EXISTS, THOUGH NO LONGER IN PLEASANT RURAL SURROUNDINGS.

THE CANDID MR BOSWELL

UNTIL THE 1920S JAMES BOSWELL WAS REMEMBERED AS THE AUTHOR OF THE MOST FAMOUS OF BRITISH BIOGRAPHIES, THE LIFE OF SAMUEL JOHNSON. THEN THE DISCOVERY OF BOSWELL'S PRIVATE JOURNALS TRANSFORMED HIS REPUTATION: FROM BEING WIDELY REGARDED AS A NAÏVE AND BUFFOONISH FIGURE, HE CAME TO BE ACKNOWLEDGED AS A GREAT SCOTTISH WRITER. BOSWELL WAS BORN IN EDINBURGH ON 29 OCTOBER 1740. HIS FATHER WAS THE LAIRD OF AUCHINLECK IN AYRSHIRE, A SUCCESSFUL LAWYER AND JUDGE, AND A SEVERE PARENT WHO HAD LITTLE UNDERSTANDING OF HIS IMAGINATIVE AND ERRATIC SON.

As a young man Boswell flirted with the theatre and Roman Catholicism and ran away for a time to London, for whose convivial and intellectual pleasures (men of distinction and women of the town) he developed a life-long passion. Back under parental control, he worked hard to pass his law examinations, and in return was allowed another trip to London, where he hoped to solicit an army commission from men of influence. He had already been exercising his gift for making friends with celebrities when, on 16 May 1763, he met Samuel Johnson, the writer he most admired.

Boswell soon overcame Johnson's anti-Scottish prejudices, and a close friendship developed in which the large, shambling, 53-year-old 'Great Cham' of English literature became a father-substitute and a role model of piety and good sense whom Boswell was comically unsuccessful in emulating. However, he had begun to write the journals in which, initially, he recorded his wide-ranging experiences of London life, including Johnson's wonderfully forceful table-talk, later to be the central feature of his biography.

Boswell's hopes of a commission proved illusory, and he reconciled himself to becoming a lawyer. After completing his studies in Holland, he went on the Grand Tour of the Continent, as was customary for young men of the upper class. He managed to meet Rousseau and Voltaire and spent a few weeks in Corsica, where Pasquale di Paoli led the resistance to Genoan, and later French, domination. Boswell's *Account of Corsica*, published in 1768, brought the hitherto-obscure

JAMES BOSWELL. THIS PORTRAIT BY GEORGE WILLISON SHOWS BOSWELL IN 1765, AT THE AGE OF TWENTY-FOUR. IT CAPTURES THE NAÏVE, ADOLESCENT QUALITY THAT COULD DESCEND INTO GAUCHENESS AND PUSHY CELEBRITY-HUNTING, BUT ALSO MADE HIM RECEPTIVE TO EVERY IMPRESSION AND ATTRACTIVE BECAUSE OF HIS APPETITE FOR EXPERIENCE.

island and its politics into the news, and for most of his life it was for this that 'Corsica Boswell' was best known.

Meanwhile he returned to Scotland in 1766 and settled down to legal practice, confining his London 'jaunts' and interviews with Johnson to vacations. His journal records the comedy of his marriage schemes, which were characteristically unrealistic or too cold-blooded for him to carry through; eventually he followed his heart and married the woman to whom he had confided them all, his cousin Margaret Montgomerie.

Boswell's career at the bar was no more than moderately successful and, having backed the wrong side in Scottish politics, his ambitions in that direction remained unfulfilled. 1773 was a red-letter year in which he was elected to The Club, a London dining society frequented by Johnson, Oliver Goldsmith, Edmund Burke, Sir Joshua Reynolds and other luminaries; it was also the year in which he persuaded Johnson to accompany him on a celebrated tour of the Hebrides. After the death of his father in 1782, the prospect of living in London became increasingly attractive, and Boswell eventually convinced himself, against all probability, that beginning in middle age he could make a new career at the English bar. The move was made in February 1786 and was materially a failure; the last nine years of Boswell's life were depressing ones in which he was abominably treated by his sole patron, the Earl of Lonsdale, his wife died, and his heavy drinking began to get out of hand.

Ironically, these were the years of Boswell's greatest literary triumphs. After Johnson's death in December 1784, he brought out his *Journal of a Tour to the Hebrides with Samuel Johnson, L.L.D.* (1785), a superbly vivid account based directly on notes made in his private journals. This was also true of the best dialogues in the great *Life of Johnson* (1791), successive editions of which occupied Boswell until his death on 19 May 1795. Boswell's distinguished friendships and literary achievements should have earned him the respect of readers, yet he was widely despised – especially by the Victorians – because of his candour in revealing his follies and fantasies and in recording Johnson's occasionally savage handling of him. The 20th century looked more tolerantly on the even greater candours of the newly discovered journals and hailed their author as one of the world's greatest literary self-portraitists.

JOHNSON AND BOSWELL IN THE HIGH STREET OF EDINBURGH, DURING THE 'JAUNT' THAT WOULD TAKE THEM THROUGH THE HIGHLANDS TO THE 'WESTERN ISLES' (THE HEBRIDES). THE FRIENDSHIP BETWEEN THE ELDERLY, SHAMBLING, PURBLIND JOHNSON AND THE EXUBERANT BOSWELL WAS A GIFT TO THE CARICATURIST, WHO IN THIS CASE WAS THOMAS ROWLANDSON.

THE ROMANCE OF HISTORY

SOME OF THE MOST ENDURING IMAGES OF SCOTLAND AND SCOTTISHNESS WERE CREATED BY AN EDINBURGH LAWYER WHO FOR YEARS REFUSED TO ACKNOWLEDGE AUTHORSHIP OF HIS EPOCH-MAKING NOVELS. SIR WALTER SCOTT EFFECTIVELY INVENTED THE HISTORICAL NOVEL, MAKING A CONSCIOUSNESS OF HISTORY A CENTRAL FEATURE OF THE ROMANTIC MOVEMENT IN THE ARTS; WITHOUT HIS EXAMPLE, THE WORKS OF DUMAS, BALZAC AND TOLSTOY WOULD HAVE BEEN VERY DIFFERENT.

And since his best works were drawn from the history of his own country, the past manners and landscapes of Scotland took on a new interest for readers all over Europe and the Americas.

Scott was born in Edinburgh on 15 August 1771. His ancestors were a border family, and at least one earlier Walter Scott was a well-known reiver. But Scott's father chose urban respectability, settling in the capital as a writer to the signet (solicitor). Young Walter was seriously ill as a child (possibly with polio), spending time in border country with his grandfather and absorbing quantities of history and folklore. Subsequently wide reading and a retentive memory provided him with more of the materials from which he would fashion splendid narratives. His illness left him lame, and although he became a remarkably active and vigorous man, he had to give up his hopes of a military career and followed his father into the law.

Scott was one of the most normal of geniuses. Popular and sociable, he drudged manfully at the law and by his mid-thirties had reached a position of comfortable affluence. After suffering a painful romantic disappointment as a young man, he married French-born Charlotte Carpenter in 1797 and, despite feelings 'something short of love in all its fervour', he remained happily married until Charlotte's death in 1826. His first publications were translations from German, followed a few years later by *Minstrelsy of the Scottish Border* (1802–3), three volumes of border ballads. Many of these were restored or reworked by Scott in a Romantic spirit that ensured their popularity with the general public. Encouraged by their reception, he began to write and pub-

SIR WALTER SCOTT, PAINTED IN 1822 BY THE DOYEN OF SCOTTISH PORTRAITISTS, SIR HENRY RAEBURN. FAMOUS IN HIS LIFETIME EVEN BEFORE HE ADMITTED THE AUTHORSHIP OF THE WAVERLEY NOVELS, SCOTT WAS FREQUENTLY SKETCHED AND PAINTED. HERE HE IS STILL AT THE HEIGHT OF HIS POWERS, BEFORE OVERWORK DESTROYED HIS HEALTH.

lish long narrative poems, set in the heroic past and full of action and colour. During the early 19th century it was possible for a poet to be a best-seller and to make a great deal of money; and Scott did both with *The Lay of the Last Minstrel* (1805), *Marmion* (1808) and other publications. The greatest success of all was *The Lady of the Lake* (1810), set around Lake Katrine and the Trossachs, which became popular early tourist areas as a direct result of Scott's influence.

His earnings enabled Scott to acquire a property on the Tweed which, by compulsive buying and building, he transformed into an antiquities-crammed mansion and estate which he named Abbotsford. There, when not busy with legal work in Edinburgh, he was able to entertain on a grand scale and act the part of a border laird.

The cost of his expensive lifestyle drove Scott to write prolifically. In 1813, recognizing that he was being eclipsed as a narrative poet by the young Lord Byron, he took up a long-abandoned novel and rapidly finished it. *Waverley*, a tale of the 1745 Jacobite rising, appeared in 1814, followed in short order by more historical novels with Scottish settings, including the works for which he is most famous, *Old Mortality*, *Rob Roy* and *The Heart of Midlothian*. From 1819 Scott also wrote, fluently though perhaps less insightfully, stories based on English history; in particular, Ivanhoe largely created the popular images of King Richard, Prince John and Robin Hood.

Waverley and its successors were issued anonymously, although the identity of the author was widely suspected and jokes circulated about 'the Great Unknown'. In 1820 he became Sir Walter Scott, Baronet, and in 1822 he organized King George IV's visit to Scotland.

Then, at the end of 1825, disaster struck. Always drawing on yet-to-be-earned income, Scott was ruined when his printers and publisher, who were in effect his business partners, went bankrupt and brought him down with them. A host of friends rallied round, but Scott vowed to work off his debts by his writings. He became more prolific than ever and earned huge sums, but his excessive labours shortened his life and led to a deterioration in his work. Following a stroke, Scott made a voyage to the Mediterranean in the hope of recovering, but after further attacks he hurried back to make his end at Abbotsford, where he died on 21 September 1832.

THE LIBRARY AT ABBOTSFORD, THE COUNTRY HOME BUILT BY SIR WALTER SCOTT WITH HIS LITERARY EARNINGS. ITS BARONIAL AIR AND THE ANTIQUARIAN NATURE OF ITS CONTENTS TESTIFY TO SCOTT'S ROMANTIC ENTHUSIASM FOR THE PAST. HIS HUGE EARNING POWER MADE HIS OVERSPENDING OF NO IMPORTANCE - UNTIL THE FINANCIAL COLLAPSE OF 1826.

SAVAGE CONFLICTS ARISE FROM ZEALOUSLY HELD BELIEFS, AS IN THIS ENGRAVING OF AN AFFRAY BETWEEN GOVERNMENT TROOPS AND COVENANTERS IN SCOTT'S NOVEL OLD MORTALITY. SCOTT'S WRITINGS CONVEY HIS MIXED FEELINGS ABOUT THE PASSIONATELY HELD BELIEFS OF THE PAST, STIRRING BUT ALSO SANGUINARY, AND THE ORDERLY, PROGRESSIVE BUT TEPID ATMOSPHERE OF HIS OWN TIME.

TELLER OF TALES

FRAIL BOHEMIAN WANDERER AND DEDICATED LITERARY CRAFTSMAN, ROBERT LOUIS STEVENSON CAPTURED THE WORLD'S IMAGINATION DURING HIS SHORT BUT INTENSELY PRODUCTIVE LIFE. HE WROTE FAST-MOVING ADVENTURES BUT ALSO CREATED CHARACTERS AND SITUATIONS NOTABLE FOR THEIR MORAL COMPLEXITY.

ROBERT LOUIS STEVENSON AND HIS WIFE FANNY IN 1887; THIS PAINTING IS BY JOHN SINGER SARGENT. STEVENSON WEARS HIS HABITUAL BOHEMIAN JACKET; FANNY, THOUGH PLACED UNOBTRUSIVELY ON THE SETTEE, IS DRESSED IN GORGEOUS INDIAN SILKS. IRONICALLY, THESE EXOTIC CREATURES WERE LIVING AT THE TIME IN THE CONVENTIONAL ENGLISH RESORT OF BOURNEMOUTH.

The one-legged sea-cook Long John Silver and the double personality of Jekyll and Hyde have become familiar to millions of readers and non-readers alike.

Born in Edinburgh on 13 November 1850, Stevenson was the son of the civil engineer Thomas Stevenson and a member of a celebrated family of lighthouse engineers. He was devotedly cared for during a sickly childhood by his nurse 'Cummie' (Alison Cunningham), whose stern religiosity left Stevenson with an ambiguous attitude towards the Scots Calvinist tradition and problems of good and evil. In 1867 he was sent to Edinburgh University to study engineering, but he was eventually allowed to change to law when it became apparent that the family profession did not attract him; he was called to the bar in 1875 but never practised. Meanwhile he took pains to learn the trade he really cared about – writing – and widened his experience by mixing with Edinburgh's low life.

During the early 1870s Stevenson's religious scepticism created difficulties with his family, on whom he was still financially dependent. Visiting a cousin in England, he developed an unrequited passion for an older woman, Frances Sitwell. He began to make a name as an essayist, writing for the leading London magazines. But his weak lungs gave cause for concern, and much of his time was spent abroad, wandering in search of health and adventure.

In 1876 Stevenson met Fanny Van de Grift Osbourne at one of his favourite haunts, the artists' colony at Grez, on the edge of the Forest of Fontainebleau south of Paris. Fanny was an independent-minded woman, ten years older than Stevenson; she was also married, though separated from her husband, and encumbered with two children. Nevertheless Stevenson was determined to marry her, and when she returned to the USA he followed her, over the ocean and across the American continent to California, in the exhausting journeys described in *The Amateur Emigrant* and *Across the Plains*. Won over, Fanny (who was now divorced) married Stevenson in May 1880, and after a romantic honeymoon in an abandoned silver miner's shack, they returned to Scotland.

At Braemar in the Highlands, Stevenson began his first novel, inspired by a pirate map he had drawn to amuse his stepson, Lloyd Osbourne. *Treasure Island* initially appeared as a serial in a children's paper with a title, *The Sea-Cook*, that focused on its villain-hero, Long John Silver. After spells in the Highlands and the South of France and winters in Davos (a well-known Swiss resort for the tubercular), the Stevensons settled in Bournemouth. In this sedate English seaside town Stevenson wrote *Kidnapped* and *Dr Jekyll and Mr Hyde*. *Kidnapped*, a historical novel set in the aftermath of the '45, follows the flight across Scotland of two friends, an uneasy partnership of Lowlander and Highlander; whereas in *Dr Jekyll and Mr Hyde* the partners are the good and evil elements in a single soul, which take on apparently separate identities while ultimately sharing a common destiny. Stevenson's powerful fable subsequently became an all-pervasive 20th-century myth.

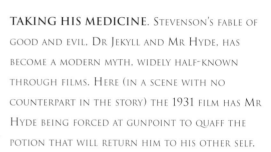

TAKING HIS MEDICINE. STEVENSON'S FABLE OF GOOD AND EVIL, DR JEKYLL AND MR HYDE, HAS BECOME A MODERN MYTH, WIDELY HALF-KNOWN THROUGH FILMS. HERE (IN A SCENE WITH NO COUNTERPART IN THE STORY) THE 1931 FILM HAS MR HYDE BEING FORCED AT GUNPOINT TO QUAFF THE POTION THAT WILL RETURN HIM TO HIS OTHER SELF.

Although creatively in full flower, Stevenson remained a sick man. After the death of his father in 1887 he took his family, including his mother, to the United States, staying in the Adirondacks, where be began another Scottish tale of division and conflict (this time between brothers), *The Master of Ballantrae*. Stevenson began his last and most exotic adventure in 1888 when he chartered a schooner and sailed for the South Seas. In 1890 he settled on Samoa and built a large wooden house which he called Vailima. His lungs improved, and he had written a substantial part of *The Weir of Hermiston*, which many critics regard as his masterpiece, when he succumbed – not to tuberculosis but to a sudden brain haemorrhage – on 3 December 1894. Well-known to the Samoans as Tusitala, 'Teller of Tales', Stevenson was carried along a path hacked through the undergrowth by friendly chiefs to a burial place on the summit of Mount Vaea.

STEVENSON IN SAMOA. THE PHOTOGRAPH SHOWS A MOUSTACHIOED STEVENSON SURROUNDED BY HIS FAMILY AND SERVANTS ON THE VERANDA OF THE HOUSE HE BUILT AT VAILIMA. INCLUDED IN THE GROUP ARE FANNY STEVENSON, HER DAUGHTER BELLE, STEVENSON'S MOTHER AND, STANDING BESIDE R.L.S., HIS STEPSON AND COLLABORATOR LLOYD OSBOURNE.

A WEALTH OF WORDS

SCOTT AND STEVENSON ARE GENERALLY REGARDED AS THE GREATEST SCOTTISH WRITERS OF THE 19TH CENTURY, BUT THERE WERE MANY OTHER GIFTED FIGURES WHOSE REPUTATIONS LIVE ON. EDINBURGH WAS A GREAT LITERARY CENTRE DURING SCOTT'S LIFETIME, HOME OF TWO OUT OF THE THREE LEADING JOURNALS OF THE DAY, THE EDINBURGH REVIEW (FOUNDED IN 1802) AND BLACKWOOD'S MAGAZINE (1819).

They have tended to be remembered by their lapses, including vicious attacks on Keats, Wordsworth and Coleridge, but they provided outlets for the work of many writers. Among these was James Hogg, known as 'the Ettrick Shepherd' because of his rural background; like Burns, he gained acceptance partly by presenting himself

as a miraculously gifted, unlettered genius. A fine poet and story-writer, Hogg is now particularly admired for his novel *The Confessions of a Justified Sinner* (1824), a highly original investigation into the dark side of the Scottish Calvinist mentality. Closely associated with Hogg on *Blackwood's* were the satirist 'Christopher North' (John Wilson) and John Gibson Lockhart, later famous for his classic biography of Sir Walter Scott.

During the first half of the century Hogg had no Scottish rivals as a poet, although his contemporary Thomas Campbell achieved great popularity with narrative battle-pieces such as 'The Battle of Hohenlinden' and the patriotic song 'Ye Mariners of England'. Later, the self-doomed, alcoholic James Thomson published *The City of Dreadful Night* (1874), in which London is the setting for verse of the bleakest pessimism. Thomson anticipated the despairs that were fashionable, though real enough, among the London decadents of the 1890s, of whom the most gifted Scottish representative was John Davidson, now remembered chiefly for his bitter tirade against poverty, 'Thirty Bob a Week'. In the starkest contrast to Davidson, William McGonagall has given unfailing entertainment to generations of readers, his *Poetic Gems* (1890) comprising verses so awful that some of them ('Railway Bridge of the Silvery Tay') have become classics of their kind.

JAMES HOGG, POET AND NOVELIST, IS PRESENTED IN THIS DRAWING AS THE AUTHOR OF 'THE CHALDEE MANUSCRIPT', A PSEUDO-ANCIENT TEXT THAT SATIRIZED THE LITERARY PERSONALITIES OF EDINBURGH. TODAY HOGG IS BEST KNOWN FOR HIS REMARKABLE PSYCHOLOGICAL-RELIGIOUS NOVEL CONFESSIONS OF A JUSTIFIED SINNER AND THE LESS CONVENTIONAL OF HIS POEMS.

A Croquis

In fiction, the century produced two gifted women writers, Susan Ferrier (*Marriage*, 1818) and Margaret Oliphant. Oliphant's need to provide for dependants accounts for her incredible productivity; she wrote a number of Scottish stories, but is now remembered for her 'Chronicles of Carlingford' series of novels about a small English country town (1861–76). John Galt's literary career was also driven by misfortune, which in his case meant a taste, but not a great capacity, for business. His fiction, by contrast, is pleasantly circumscribed in scope: his best-known novel, *Annals of the Parish* (1822), is a straightforward, touching description of the life of a minister in a small Ayrshire town. By contrast, George Macdonald was a real (Congregational) minister whose principal gift was for fantasy, although he wrote in several genres after giving up the ministry in 1855; despite some shortcomings, *Phantastes* (1858) and *Lilith* (1895) are works of unusual imaginative power, and *At the Back of the North Wind* (1871) and other children's books by Macdonald are still recognized as classics.

During the Victorian period and for some time afterwards, most readers and critics would have named Thomas Carlyle, 'the sage of Eccelfechan', as the century's greatest Scottish author. Struggling against poverty, he popularized German literature through essays and translations, before establishing himself as a moral-literary force with works such as the eccentric *Sartor Resartus* (1835), *On Heroes and Hero-Worship* (lectures, published in 1841), and *The French Revolution* (1837) and other historical studies. Carlyle was a preacher, but he put forward no religious doctrine, confining himself to an affirmation of values such as personal integrity, hard work and duty; this was probably the secret of his appeal to Victorian intellectuals who had lost their faith while still feeling the need for a sense of moral purpose. But although he sometimes rose to heights of almost mystical eloquence in describing his personal vision, later generations became less enthusiastic about his too-cloudy creed, his cult of the great man, and his sinewy, consciously Germanic style. Still regarded as important, and reappraised from time to time, his work has so far failed to win back ordinary readers.

THE BOY DIAMOND ENCOUNTERS THE NORTH WIND: ONE OF THE ILLUSTRATIONS BY THE PRE-RAPHAELITE ARTIST ARTHUR HUGHES TO GEORGE MACDONALD'S CHILDREN'S CLASSIC AT THE BACK OF THE NORTH WIND. PUBLISHED IN 1871, THE STORY COMBINED ELEMENTS OF SOCIAL REALISM (THE TRIBULATIONS OF POOR FAMILIES) WITH CHARMING FANTASY AND SUBTLE SYMBOLISM.

Readers have never been wanting for the works of Sir Arthur Conan Doyle, the Edinburgh-born physician who wrote while vainly waiting for patients to find their way to his Southsea practice. Prolific and hugely popular, he wrote novels and stories in many genres and became a public figure, committed to the imperial ideals of late Victorian Britain; significantly, his historical novels evoke the medieval past of England, not Scotland. He believed these were his master-works and would have been disappointed to know that, at the end of the millennium, he still owed his fame to his immortal supersleuth, Sherlock

Holmes. Conan Doyle's fellow-Scot, J.M. Barrie, was also popular and successful. He was the chief representative of what was dubbed (in derision) the Kailyard school – the kailyard, or cabbage patch, symbolizing the small Scots village or town, described with cloying sentimentality and with enough in the way of Scotticisms to charm Anglo-Saxon readers without putting them off. Barrie also made a separate reputation as a popular London playwright. His most frequently revived play is *The Admirable Crichton* (1902), based on the observation that, stranded on a desert island, the butler may well be a better man than the duke; but the perennial favourite among his works is *Peter Pan* (1904), a pantomime about 'the boy who never grew up', in which sentimentality is relieved by surreal humour as the villain, Captain Hook, is pursued by a crocodile whose presence is given away by the alarm clock in its interior. An equally successful Scot, John Buchan, ended as a peer and governor-general of Canada. His most enduring books are thrillers, beginning with *The Thirty-Nine Steps* (1915) and *Greenmantle* (1916), in which the engineer hero Richard Hannay battles against fiendishly subversive plots; these have proved gripping enough to preserve the books despite their often obnoxious prejudices. The period following the First World War of 1914–18 is often described in literary terms as the Scottish Renaissance. Its leading figure was Hugh MacDiarmid, a poet whose most original works were written in a form of Scots partly of his own devising, which he called Synthetic Scots or Lallans (Lowlands). MacDiarmid's finest Scots poem was *A Drunk Man Looks at the Thistle* (1926); his work combined modernist sophistication with a combative literary attitude towards the 'English ascendancy' and erratic political commitments to Scottish Nationalism and Communism. A number of poets were inspired by MacDiarmid to write in Scots, among them William Soutar and Sydney Goodsir Smith. The leading Scottish Renais-

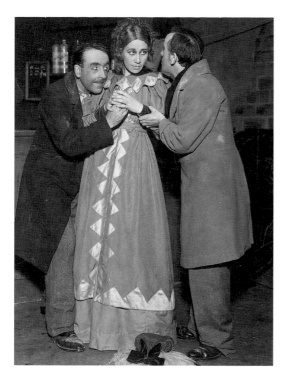

WITH MURDER IN MIND: A SCENE FROM JAMES BRIDIE'S PLAY THE ANATOMIST AS PRESENTED AT WESTMINSTER IN 1931. IT EXTRACTS GRIM COMEDY FROM THE EXPLOITS OF THE MURDERERS BURKE AND HARE, WHO PERPETRATED THEIR CRIMES IN ORDER TO SELL THE BODIES OF THEIR VICTIMS TO AN EDINBURGH ANATOMIST FOR DISSECTION.

sance novelists were Neil M. Gunn and Lewis Grassic Gibbon, both of whom wrote of their native north-east. Gunn was long-lived and wrote widely, often in mystical vein, as well as publishing regional works such as *Highland River* (1937) and *The Silver Darlings* (1941). Grassic Gibbon died at thirty-four, writing prolifically in the last six years of his life after years spent in the army and RAF. His trilogy *A Scots Quair* (1932–4) narrates the life of a woman, Chris Guthrie, who moves between rural and urban, industrial Scotland; the latter had previously been given remarkably little attention in the Scottish novel, with its tradition of village and small-town tales. Another aspect of the 'Renaissance' was a Gaelic revival. In the 18th century Gaelic poetry had proved to be surprisingly vigorous, finding new subjects as the bardic tradition decayed. Anger and nostalgia – responses to the Clearances and internal or foreign exile – dominated 19th-century writing. In the 20th century, however, despite the shrinking numbers of Gaelic speakers, major poets appeared in Sorley Maclean, considered by many the finest poet ever to have written in the language, and George Campbell Hay. Magazines, radio and later television provided channels which enabled short-story writing to flourish, and the leading present-day writer in Gaelic, Iain Crichton Smith, has published novels as well as stories and poems in the language. Writing in English remained vigorous. Admired poets included Edwin Muir, Norman MacCaig, G.S. Fraser, W.S. Graham and Edwin Morgan. The novelist Sir Compton Mackenzie enjoyed an exceptionally long career: he had already published a great deal when he wrote *Sinister Street* (1913–14), still highly regarded as an example of the type of novel in which a young person is educated by sobering encounters with the world outside academe. Mackenzie's own experiences provided him with a wealth of materials for novels, culminating in old age with comic narratives based in the Highlands and Islands; the best-known is certainly *Whisky Galore* (1947).

Scotland produced another important playwright in James Bridie. His career was helped by the Scottish National Players, a theatre group founded in 1921, but in general theatrical life in Scotland remained disappointingly sluggish until after the Second World War.

TRAINSPOTTING. THIS STILL FROM THE 1995 FILM, WITH EWEN MCGREGOR AS RENTON, WAS USED FOR THE POSTER ADVERTISING IT AND BECAME ONE OF THE MOST FAMILIAR IMAGES OF THE LATE 1990S. THE FILM WAS BASED ON A NOVEL BY IRVINE WELSH WHICH GIVES AN UNSPARING ACCOUNT OF ALIENATION AND HEROIN ADDICTION AMONG THE YOUNG IN CONTEMPORARY EDINBURGH.

ARTS AND ENTERTAINMENT

ABOVE: The Lude Harp, a traditional Scottish instrument (left) and Edinburgh from Calton Hill; painting by David Roberts

THE SWORD DANCE, vigorously performed by a competitor at a Highland Games. The multiplication of Games, which combine athletic events with music and dancing competitions, has helped to maintain interest in the folk tradition in the Highlands. The sword dance involves intricate steps over and around swords arranged on the ground. Its origin is unknown, but it is certainly over two centuries old

TRUTHFUL PORTRAITS AND ATMOSPHERIC
    LANDSCAPES HAVE BEEN AMONG THE FINEST
ACHIEVEMENTS OF SCOTTISH PAINTING.
    STRONG FOLK TRADITIONS HAVE ENLIVENED
MUSIC AND DANCING, AND SCOTTISH ACTORS
    AND COMEDIANS HAVE BEEN WELL AND
WIDELY LOVED.

THE EARLY CENTURIES

THANKS TO WARS, BANDITRY AND THE ZEAL OF THE PROTESTANT REFORMERS WHO SMASHED IDOLATROUS IMAGES AND OBJECTS, RELATIVELY LITTLE SCOTTISH ART SURVIVES FROM BEFORE ABOUT 1600. FROM WHAT REMAINS, IT IS OFTEN IMPOSSIBLE TO TRACE LINES OF DEVELOPMENT OR EVEN TO DISTINGUISH BETWEEN NATIVE WORKS AND FOREIGN IMPORTS.

It is therefore all the more surprising to find a sudden flowering in the 18th century, when Scotland produced several painters of European stature, followed by two centuries of solid achievement within an identifiably national tradition.

Though Scots are proud of the fact that the Romans never conquered (much of) their country, some of the earliest works of art were made by Roman, or Roman-trained, craftsmen; one of the most striking is a funerary monument showing a lioness devouring a man, discovered in 1997 at Cramond on the south bank of the Forth, once the site of a fort and harbour used to supply the Antonine Wall. Most of the artefacts left by the Romans' enemies, the Picts, were made much later, between the 7th and 10th centuries. Apart from a few gold and silver ornaments, the main evidence of Pictish culture comes from standing stones carved with varying degrees of sophistication; the most thoroughly worked are rectangular slabs with scenes in relief, the distinctive symbols used by the Picts, and the Christian cross.

Pictish designs are obviously, if obscurely, related to the 'Celtic' art associated with the Irish, the Dalriada Scots and the non-Romanized Britons. Featuring fluent, often intertwining lines, sometimes geometric in form and sometimes incorporating plants and animals, Celtic art is celebrated for beautiful metalwork and illuminated manuscripts; although their geographical origin can be hard to place, some items are definitely Scottish and, more controversially, Scotland can lay claim to the famous Book of Kells, believed to have been created on the island of Iona.

Scotland's Norse heritage is represented by the chessmen made of walrus ivory, found

THE RUTHWELL CROSS DATES FROM THE 8TH CENTURY AND CARRIES EXCELLENT CARVINGS OF BIBLICAL SCENES ALONG WITH LATIN AND RUNIC INSCRIPTIONS. IT WAS ALMOST CERTAINLY THE WORK OF A NORTHUMBRIAN ANGLE (A REMINDER THAT THIS PEOPLE CONTRIBUTED TO THE SCOTTISH RACIAL MIX), ALTHOUGH ITS FIRST KNOWN LOCATION WAS RUTHWELL IN DUMFRIESSHIRE.

in the sand on the Isle of Lewis in 1831; the combination of military detail with apparently staring eyes gives them a peculiar intensity, qualified by the humour with which a shield-gnawing warrior-pawn is carved.

Much of Scotland's medieval art exists only in a fragmentary state, with magnificent ruins such as the great Cistercian abbeys still standing to hint at what has been lost. For centuries, foreign works and foreign craftsmen seem to have been imported on an increasing scale; an outstanding example is the altarpiece originally in the Trinity College Church, Edinburgh, with a portrait of James III and his queen, which is attributed to the great Netherlandish painter Hugo van der Goes. Although James IV is known to have appointed a Scottish court painter, George Jameson is the first named Scottish artist whose paintings (other than manuscript illuminations) have survived. He worked in his native Aberdeen, but was sufficiently well known to be summoned to Edinburgh to assist in the preparations for Charles I's arrival in 1633. On this occasion he painted a series of imaginary royal portraits, but his best work is in true portraiture; and he also painted self-portraits, including one with his easel, showing that the Renaissance artist's consciousness of vocation had already reached Scotland.

Jameson remained an exceptional figure, mainly because in Scotland patronage of the arts was limited after 1603, when James VI and his

KNIGHT, QUEEN AND BISHOP, THREE PIECES FROM THE CACHE OF CHESSMEN DISCOVERED IN 1831 ON THE SOUTH SHORE OF UIG BAY ON THE ISLE OF LEWIS. 12TH-CENTURY NORSE WORK, THESE EXPRESSIVE OBJECTS ARE CARVED FROM WALRUS IVORY; THE 78 KNOWN PIECES ARE DIVIDED BETWEEN THE BRITISH MUSEUM AND THE MUSEUM OF SCOTLAND.

court departed for London; Jameson's most important pupil, John Michael Wright, made his career abroad. The civil wars and the Restoration were followed by the 1707 Act of Union, which led to an even greater exodus to the south, and a gifted portraitist such as William Aikman was compelled to seek his fortune in London. Even as Scotland entered the great age of the Enlightenment, Allan Ramsay, the country's first indisputably great painter, set up his studio in London in 1739. During the middle decades of the century he dominated portraiture, balancing lightness and gravity in a highly distinctive fashion. Fortunately, despite his London residence he was able to work frequently in Scotland, creating definitive images of leading figures such as the philosopher David Hume (1766).

Ramsay was the outstanding portraitist of his generation, but he had a number of talented contemporaries, including Catherine Read, the first Scottish woman to establish herself as a professional painter. But the greatest international reputation of the period belonged to the now less esteemed Gavin Hamilton. Like Ramsay and many others, he studied in Italy, but after practising as a portraitist in London he was drawn back to Rome in the 1760s, where as artist, excavator of Roman remains and picture dealer he was a central figure in the Neo-Classical revival based on a combination of moral earnestness and an antiquarian approach to history. *Achilles Lamenting the Death of Patroclus* (1763)

MARGARET LYNDSAY, THE WIFE OF THE ARTIST ALLAN RAMSAY, WHO PAINTED THIS PORTRAIT OF HER IN 1754-55. NO DOUBT BECAUSE OF ITS SUBJECT, IT IS MORE INFORMAL THAN MOST OF RAMSAY'S PORTRAITS, BUT IT IS OTHERWISE CHARACTERISTIC IN THE WAY IT COMBINES DELICACY OF TOUCH WITH QUIET CHARM AND A MUTED GRAVITY.

and other large paintings by Hamilton now seem frigidly melodramatic, but his historical importance was considerable.

Scottish portraiture reached its apogee in the work of Henry Raeburn, who was initially apprenticed to a goldsmith and painted miniatures before turning to easel painting. After belated studies in Italy, at the age of thirty-one he settled in Edinburgh (1787), becoming the first Scottish artist to acquire wide recognition while remaining firmly based in his native land. His spontaneous, forceful style was based on painting directly on to the canvas without making preliminary drawings, the broadly painted areas serving to heighten Raeburn's use of vivid, telling detail. Encompassing the intimate and the grandly formal, Raeburn painted a cross-section of wealthy Scots society, not omitting scarlet-coated military men and Highland chiefs enriched by the Clearances but flaunting their traditional role, now viewed through the romantic nostalgia so effectively promoted by Raeburn's friend Sir Walter Scott. However, modern packaging and image-making has ensured that the gravely informal painting of *Rev. Robert Walker Skating* (*c*.1784) has become the most popular of all his paintings.

Whereas portraiture had long been recognized as a 'fine' art, the Scottish landscape tradition developed out of a humbler jobbing background: the made-to-order scenes required to fill niches in the

Neo-Classical interiors that were being designed for an increasingly wealthy upper class. The specialists in this department were the Norrie family, whose apprentices, Alexander Runciman and Jacob More, emerged as independent artists from the 1760s. Their example was followed by Alexander Nasmyth, who began as studio assistant to Ramsay in London, worked as a portraitist in Edinburgh, but then turned to landscape after returning from Italy in 1785. He painted in the classical tradition associated with the French artist Claude, side-framing his scenes in theatrical style while imbuing them with a sense of radiant harmony; but although, in 18th-century fashion, he often spiced his compositions with caprices (imaginary architectural features), he gave considerable attention to observed details and produced a number of evocative Edinburgh cityscapes. Nasmyth fostered youthful talent, encouraging his acolytes to sketch from nature; the most successful, James Thomson, developed a more emotional and dramatic style, characteristically displayed in wild Highland studies such as *Glencoe* (1804).

A very different type of Scottish scene gained in popularity towards the end of the 18th century. Paintings showing episodes of daily life, usually among humble people, are known as genre; they were a speciality of 17th-century Dutch artists, and seem to have had a particular appeal to Scots as they developed a prosperous middle-class society not unlike that of the Netherlands.

The first important practitioner, David Allan, seems to have taken up genre partly because there was so little interest in grand historical subjects; his rather naïve style gives charm to works such as *The Penny Wedding* (1795). Genre was taken to London by David Wilkie, whose *Village Politicians* (1806) was an immediate and overwhelming success. Mixing humour with 'serious' social comment in works such as *The Refusal* (1814), he was probably the most admired British painter until the 1820s, when he tried to escape from his self-created stereotypes by changes of style and subject. Wilkie's influence on 19th-century art was profound, since his works were largely responsible for creating an enduring Victorian market for anecdotal painting.

THE SKATING CLERGYMAN HAS BECOME THE MOST CELEBRATED OF RAEBURN'S PORTRAITS. WALKER'S RATHER STIFF AND SOLEMN GAIT MAKES A NICE CONTRAST WITH HIS FRIVOLOUS PURSUIT; AND PICTORIALLY THE LARGE AREAS OF CLERICAL BLACK, RELIEVED ONLY BY THE WHITE SCARF AT WALKER'S THROAT, STAND OUT WITH SPLENDID CLARITY AGAINST THE MISTY NATURAL SETTING.

MODERN MOVEMENTS

DURING THE HIGH VICTORIAN PERIOD, SCOTTISH
ARTISTS PRODUCED A RESPECTABLE BODY OF WORK IN
THE RECEIVED STYLES OF HISTORY PAINTING, GENRE
AND LANDSCAPE. HOWEVER, MORE ORIGINAL EFFECTS
WERE OFTEN ACHIEVED WHEN THEY TURNED AWAY
FROM THEIR ACCUSTOMED SUBJECTS; OUTSTANDING
EXAMPLES ARE WILLIAM DYCE'S PEGWELL BAY, KENT
(1859–60) AND OTHER LANDSCAPES PAINTED TOWARDS
THE END OF THE ARTIST'S LIFE; IN THESE, HIS RELIGIOUS
PREOCCUPATIONS COMBINED WITH HIS MASTERY
OF NATURALISTIC DETAIL TO CREATE HAUNTINGLY
BEAUTIFUL SCENES.

THE FIRST CLOUD BY SIR WILLIAM ORCHARDSON.
APPARENTLY CONVENTIONAL IN TREATMENT,
ORCHARDSON'S PAINTING ACHIEVES AN UNUSUAL
EFFECT BY USING PHYSICAL SPACE TO INDICATE
PSYCHOLOGICAL DISTANCE. THE UPPER-CLASS SETTING,
EVOKING CODES OF FORMALITY AND RESTRAINT,
ENABLES THE ARTIST TO REPRESENT A FALLING-OUT
WITHOUT ANY OVERT ACTION TAKING PLACE.

Though Wilkie's reception in London
encouraged his many Scottish imitators to
move south, none enjoyed any notable success. By contrast, from the 1860s William
Quiller Orchardson made a triumphant career
in England by producing a new kind of genre
which replaced the humble cottage with the
upper-class drawing room. Works such as *The
First Cloud* (1887) feature sumptuous set-
tings and couples who are dressed in the height of elegance; but the
gloss of their existence only emphasizes their emotional alienation,

made plain by the interesting pictorial device of separating them by daringly large spaces.

Orchardson was one of a gifted generation of students who graduated in the 1850s from the Trustees' Academy, Edinburgh, at that time the premier teaching institution. The Academy's pupils also included William McTaggart, who was born in Campbelltown and found his best subjects in his native Highlands. His early paintings were in the genre tradition of Wilkie, but during the 1860s he turned increasingly to landscape, painting in a style that was more free than the tight, precise manner prescribed by convention. He also did much of his work out of doors, in the form of sketches and oil studies (to be worked up later in his studio), to an extent that was then unusual. (Painting the picture itself out of doors was unheard of in Britain until a generation or so after the practice was introduced by the French Impressionists in the 1870s.) McTaggart's choice of grand dramatic subjects, such as *The Storm* (1890), helped to make his work relatively popular in spite of its unorthodox elements; it also appears that he was not without commercial guile, deliberately inserting picturesque details at a late stage in his work to ensure that it appealed to the substantial art-buying public of late-Victorian Scotland.

McTaggart's interest in the handling of paint, and in light effects and atmosphere, were symptoms of a growing reaction against Victorian academicism. In the 1880s a group of artists nicknamed the Glasgow Boys rejected the sentimental and anecdotal genre tradition, painting soberly realistic pictures of rustic life such as James Guthrie's *The Hind's Daughter* (1884); two of the younger Glasgow Boys, George Henry and E.A. Hornel, evolved a more decorative, patterned style that was even more unconventional. New institutions were also heralds of change: in 1891 the organization of a Society of Scottish Artists broke the Scottish Royal Academy's monopoly as an exhibiting society, and the founding

PORT SETON, BY WILLIAM MCTAGGART. ESSENTIALLY A FINE, ATMOSPHERIC SHORE- AND SEASCAPE, THE PAINTING ALSO INCORPORATED ENOUGH IN THE WAY OF HUMAN INTEREST (BOATS AND PEOPLE, INCLUDING CHILDREN) TO ENSURE THAT IT APPEALED TO A VICTORIAN PUBLIC.

BUTTERFLY FLOWER, BY CHARLES RENNIE MACKINTOSH AND HIS WIFE MARGARET MACDONALD; ONE OF THEIR MANY WATERCOLOUR FLOWER STUDIES, THIS ONE WAS DONE AT BOWLING, ON THE CLYDE, IN 1912. MORE FAMOUS AS AN ARCHITECT AND DESIGNER, C.R. MACKINTOSH RETURNED TO PAINTING, IN A DISTINCTIVE MODERN STYLE, IN HIS LAST YEARS.

REFLECTIONS, BALLOCH: A PAINTING (C.1929) BY G. LESLIE HUNTER, ONE OF THE SCOTTISH COLOURISTS WHO STUDIED IN PARIS AND ABSORBED THE LESSONS OF FRENCH IMPRESSIONISM AND POST-IMPRESSIONISM. HERE BALLOCH - A PLEASURE RESORT AND BOATING CENTRE ON LOCH LOMOND – HAS A DISTINCTLY CONTINENTAL AIR.

of art schools created a favourable environment for lively-minded teachers and students. This was especially true of the Glasgow School of Art, which fostered the talents of the now internationally famous Charles Rennie Mackintosh. Mackintosh's greatest achievements were as an architect and designer, but he was also a gifted poster artist and watercolour painter. In the early 1890s, at the Glasgow School of Art, he was closely associated with three fellow-students, the sisters Margaret and Frances Macdonald and Herbert MacNair. The 'Glasgow Four' responded to the end-of-the-century Symbolist and Art Nouveau trends, with their air of mystery, fluent lines and flattened, decorative motifs, but they added to it their own dash of Celtic mysticism. The Macdonalds created strange, skeletal figures that caused the sisters to be nicknamed 'the spooks'; Mackintosh's more restrained mysticism appears in paintings such as *The Harvest Moon* (1892). During his creative period as an architect, Margaret Macdonald, who became his wife, designed many of the figurative elements in his designs, but Mackintosh returned to painting when his career faltered, creating beautiful, stylized, highly individual-flower pieces and, later, watercolours of the landscapes and harbours of the South of France.

After 1900, Scottish painters became aware that a series of artistic revolutions were taking place on the Continent, and of these the liberation of colour became a particularly strong influence on Scottish art all through the 20th century. The first to be seriously affected were a group of young painters now known as the Scottish Colourists: J.D. Fergusson, S.J. Peploe, F.C.B. Cadell and G. Leslie Hunter, all of whom worked for considerable periods in France before returning to Scotland. The early works of Peploe and Fergusson were influenced by the still lifes of Manet, but all four of the group were overwhelmed by the bold, non-naturalistic colour of the Fauves, who burst upon the Paris scene in 1905, and in particular by Henri Matisse in both his Fauve and his more decorative phases. The Colourists produced many stylish works that were rich in colour and decorative appeal, even if their French inspiration was apparent. Cadell was perhaps the most successful in translating French influences into a native idiom, notably in his drawing-room scenes, portraits and Iona landscapes. Fergusson was the most ambitious, at one point attempting to combine rich colour with a stylized monumentality, for example in *At My Studio Window* (1910). He was also the most influential of the group, partly thanks to his longevity (1874–1961), which gave him the status of the Grand Old Man of Modernism after he settled in Glasgow in 1939.

After 1918, depression years and the rise of photography meant that there was less demand for portraits and conventional views – the paradoxical result being that artists, no longer in receipt of regular commissions, gained a new freedom to experiment. In any case there was no longer a single dominant style, and in the decades that followed, Scottish artists adopted and adapted everything from machine-minded Futurism and Vorticism to irreverent and dream-driven Surrealism. Of the many interwar figures, the most prominent were members of the 'Edinburgh school', including William Gilles, William Johnstone, Anne Redpath and John Maxwell. From the 1940s, leading artists tended to be absorbed into the London or even the international art world. 'The Roberts' – Robert Colquhoun and Robert MacBryde – made a considerable impact on the 1940s London art scene until a change in fashion and their self-destructive impulses caused them to sink into obscurity. The Glasgow-born and self-taught Scottie Wilson was a still more eccentric, tramp-like figure, but his staying power was greater and his decorative fantasies remained popular from the late 1930s until his death in 1972.

Scottish art has flourished since the Second World War. Joan Eardley, who was Scottish by adoption, painted powerful, bleak, land- and sea-scapes, based on views of the north-east coast but verging on abstraction. William Gear made an international reputation with abstract paintings, typically with colours organized by a superimposed grid. The best-known Scottish artists at the end of the 20th century were Ian Hamilton Finlay, Alan Davie and Sir Eduardo Paolozzi. Ian Hamilton Finlay, originally best known as a poet, has devoted himself to his Pentland Hills garden, in which objects and inscriptions are scattered, surprising the viewer by incongruous juxtapositions and visual and verbal puns. Alan Davie has worked mainly in London and, more recently, on St Lucia in the Caribbean; influenced by primitive art and Buddhism, his paintings combine real and imaginary signs and images to create a sense of magical forces at work.

Eduardo Paolozzi was born in Edinburgh of Italian parents and studied at the Edinburgh College of Art and the Slade School, London. In the late 1940s he began making collages; in retrospect, his use of materials such as American magazines was the most important aspect of this activity, anticipating the Pop Art movement in incorporating 'non-art' imagery generated by popular culture. He then concentrated mainly on sculpture, producing machine-like objects which later became highly colourful and acquired a 'primitive' aura. Among his best-known public commissions are mosaic decorations for Tottenham Court Road Underground station (1983–5) and the huge bronze *Wealth of Nations* (1993) at South Gyle, Edinburgh. Though most of Paolozzi's work has been done outside Scotland, his achievement is commemorated in the Paolozzi Foundation, Edinburgh.

BASH. A 1971 PRINT BY SIR EDUARDO PAOLOZZI, PROBABLY SCOTLAND'S BEST-KNOWN CONTEMPORARY ARTIST. IT BRINGS TOGETHER A RANGE OF FAMILIAR MASS-MEDIA IMAGERY (MARILYN MONROE, AN ASTRONAUT) IN POP ART STYLE. IN 1999 THE CONTENTS OF PAOLOZZI'S STUDIO BECAME THE BASIS OF THE NEW DEAN GALLERY IN EDINBURGH.

MUSIC-MAKERS AND PERFORMERS

MUSICAL INSTRUMENTS SURVIVE FROM PREHISTORIC SCOTLAND, THE EARLIEST BEING A FRAGMENT FROM THE 8TH CENTURY BC. PICTISH STONE CARVINGS PRESERVE IMAGES OF TRUMPET, HARP, PIPE AND DRUM FROM ABOUT THE 8TH CENTURY AD, AND ROUGHLY CONTEMPORARY IRON AND BRONZE HAND BELLS, USED IN CELTIC CHRISTIAN SERVICES, SURVIVE IN GOOD CONDITION.

CHORAL MUSIC: A PAGE FROM THE EARLY 16TH-CENTURY CARVER CHOIRBOOK. CONSISTING OF FIVE MASSES AND TWO MOTETS OF GREAT BEAUTY AND TECHNICAL SKILL, THE MANUSCRIPT IS A RARE SURVIVING EXAMPLE OF SCOTTISH POLYPHONIC MUSIC FROM THE PRE-REFORMATION PERIOD. THE COMPOSITIONS ARE ATTRIBUTED TO ROBERT CARVER, THE CANON OF SCONE ABBEY.

The earliest Scottish musical manuscripts date from the 13th century. The subsequent music of church and court had a chequered history, with major interruptions in the tradition, brought about by the Wars of Independence, the Reformation and the removal of the court to London in 1603. Scotland has produced some fine composers in the European tradition, from Robert Carver in the 16th century to Thea Musgrave and David Dorward in the 20th; but it must be admitted that Scotland's vocal and instrumental folk music has been more distinctive and has had a wider impact on non-Scottish sensibilities.

Gaelic music was closely connected with poetic recitations by the bards and the later poets who composed in less 'classical' language. Most Gaelic poetry was intended to be sung, but none of the music for it was written down until the 18th century; some of these orally preserved materials are nevertheless very old. Among them are songs said to have been composed by fairies, mainly describing their love affairs with mortals, and work songs that lightened and co-ordinated collective labours; the best-known are the waulking songs sung when beating cloth.

The first collection of Gaelic songs was published in 1784. By contrast, Scots songs began to appear in print, initially in English collections, from the mid-17th century, and half a

century earlier there were already enthusiasts compiling manuscript collections. From the 18th century, many traditional airs were rescued by poets – above all by Robert Burns – who wrote lyrics for them. Meanwhile folk songs continued to be composed, especially in response to the 1745 Jacobite rising, ranging from 'Hey, Johnnie Cope', jeering at the Hanoverian general caught napping at Prestonpans, to the mournful 'Will ye no' come back again?' Ballad collecting was also keenly pursued in the 18th century, but words rather than music interested compilers like Sir Walter Scott (whose celebrated *Minstrelsy of the Scottish Border*, 1803, seems to have given rise to the illusion that all Scots ballads were composed in the borders). Attempts to recover the music began much later, but proved very successful.

DR FINLAY'S CASEBOOK, AN IMMENSELY POPULAR TELEVISION SERIES OF THE 1960s, WAS BASED ON THE WRITINGS OF THE DOCTOR-NOVELIST A.J. CRONIN AND CHRONICLED WITH GENTLE HUMOUR THE DOINGS OF YOUNG SMALL-TOWN DOCTOR FINLAY (BILL SIMPSON, RIGHT), HIS TESTY SENIOR PARTNER DR CAMERON (ANDREW CRUIKSHANK) AND THEIR NO-NONSENSE HOUSEKEEPER JANET (BARBARA MULLEN).

COUNTRY DANCING PERFORMED IN PUBLIC AT KELSO. THIS POPULAR PURSUIT IS MISNAMED: 'COUNTRY' IS A CORRUPTION OF THE FRENCH WORD *CONTRE*, AGAINST OR OPPOSITE, DESCRIBING THE WAY IN WHICH THE LINES OF DANCERS ARE ARRANGED IN PAIRS, FACING EACH OTHER; THEY PERFORM SOME STEPS INDIVIDUALLY AND OTHERS AS PARTNERS.

Three instruments are closely associated with Scottish traditional music: the harp, the bagpipes and the fiddle. The harp is certainly the oldest; it is pictured on carved Pictish stones from the 8th century, by which time it had probably spread to Gaelic areas in the west. The Gaelic harp, or clarsach, was triangular, stood on an upright fore-pillar, and was strung with wire. It accompanied the effusions of the bards, and declined along with the clan system, effectively disappearing after 1745 – so completely that certainly authentic early music for the clarsach has not survived. Revived late in the 19th century, the instrument has featured regularly at the chief Gaelic musical festival, the National Mod, and has gained a loyal following.

The place of the harp as the national instrument was taken by the bagpipes, an instrument that is sometimes mistakenly believed to be uniquely Scottish, although it is in fact found in a number of cultures. The Lowland bagpipes, worked with a bellows, has disappeared along with any music composed for it. The type with which everyone is familiar is the Highland bagpipes, in which the air is supplied by the piper's breath and expelled by the pressure of the elbow on the bag. Bagpipes are first documented in the 16th century, and may or may not be significantly older than that. Though played as an accompaniment to dances or marching, for example by pipe bands, they attain their full dignity as solo instruments performing pibroch, essentially a set of ornate variations on a theme which gives the piper an opportunity for virtuoso display. Pibroch is said to have been invented by Donald Mor MacCrimmon (*c*.1570–1640), founder of a piping dynasty which served the MacLeod chiefs for centuries.

Like other symbols of the clan way of life, the bagpipes were proscribed after the failure of the '45, but the Highland regiments were exempted from the ban and ensured their survival into a more sympathetic era.

Whereas the bagpipes were mainly Highland instruments, fiddles and fiddle music were in evidence all over Scotland. The range and liveliness of the fiddle made it a popular favourite, especially as an accompaniment to dancing. Its appeal to ordinary people, improvising a dance in a cottage, is obvious; but it enjoyed a wider vogue in the sociable 18th century, when the most gifted fiddlers were patronized by the aristocracy and recorded or composed quantities of songs and airs as well as tunes for reels, jigs and other forms of Scottish country dancing. Niel Gow and his son Nathaniel Gow were the dominant figures for almost a century from the mid-1700s, despite competition from William Marshall and other composer-executants; the Gows' compositions, some of them quietly appropriated from older sources, provided their successors with an abundant repertoire of melodies and dance tunes, added to in very recent times by James Scott Skinner (1843–1927).

The vigorous folk-music tradition helped to make dancing a popular Scottish pastime. In set dances such as reels, two lines of dancers face each other, performing some steps individually and others with their partners. This is Scottish country dancing – 'country' being a corruption of *contre*, French for 'against' (signifying opposite). There are also dances involving couples, including the celebrated Gay Gordons, and solo performances such as the Sword Dance and the Highland Fling. The specifically

'THEY LOVE ME IN MY KILT!' COMEDIAN-SINGER HARRY LAUDER ADOPTED A NUMBER OF MOCK-SCOTTISH COSTUMES DURING HIS CAREER, BUT HE IS BEST REMEMBERED AS THE KILTED HIGHLANDER WITH A KNOBBLY STICK, CRACKING JOKES BETWEEN RENDITIONS OF PERENNIAL FAVOURITES SUCH AS 'THE ROAD TO THE ISLES' AND 'ROAMIN' IN THE GLOAMIN'.

MRS BROWN (1997) WAS ONE OF THE MOST-PRAISED FILMS OF THE 1990S, FEATURING JUDI DENCH AS THE WIDOWED QUEEN VICTORIA AND BILLY CONNOLLY AS HER OUTSPOKEN SCOTTISH SERVANT, JOHN BROWN. IT DESCRIBES THE CLOSE RELATIONSHIP BETWEEN THE TWO, THE CONSEQUENT RUMOURS, AND BROWN'S ROLE IN THE QUEEN'S RETURN TO PUBLIC LIFE.

Highland aspects of traditional dancing are nurtured by competitions at the Highland Games. In terms of its music, the most original dance is the Strathspey reel, characterized by 'the Scotch Snap': a short note on the beat, followed by a longer note sustained until the next beat begins; it is found in well-known songs such as 'Comin' through the Rye'.

For a long time the 'serious' Scottish theatre had little to distinguish it from its English counterpart. Much more of the national vitality went into the music halls and variety theatres, whose performers became the folk heroes of the 19th and 20th centuries. The advent of the wireless and records preserved the personalities of figures such as the comedian Will Fyffe and, above all, Harry Lauder, who became an international star performing in the comic-sentimental character of a Highlander; though the stereotype he created has sometimes irritated Scots, songs such as 'Roamin' in the Gloamin'' and 'Keep Right on to the End of the Road' have proved enduringly popular.

The variety tradition persisted until the post-Second World War period, giving their first chance to performers such as Stanley Baxter and Andy Stewart who later made their mark in television. Others established their reputations in films, usually followed by excursions into television; in these media, actors such as Gordon Jackson and John Laurie, though gifted, tended to be type-cast (as, respectively, upright, respectable Scot and mildly unhinged prophet of doom). In recent times, less programmed attitudes have enabled Sean Connery not only to play a suave, Scottish James Bond, but to become a versatile international superstar; and though the comedian Billy Connolly makes greater play with his Scottish persona as 'the Big Yin' (the Big One), he too has had acting opportunities denied to performers of earlier generations.

Economic realities have made it impossible for a Scottish film industry to develop, and producers and directors, like actors, have had to make their careers in England or abroad. Perhaps the most influential figure of all was John Grierson, who both coined the term 'documentary' and pioneered the genre as director, producer and theoretician. Under his aegis a group of talented documentarists emerged (including a Scottish director, Harry Watt) at the Empire Marketing Board and GPO Film Unit, where classics such as *Song of Ceylon* (1934) and *Night Mail* (1936) were made; and among Grierson's notable later achievements was the establishment of the National Film Board of Canada.

BUILDINGS & MONUMENTS

ABOVE: THREAVE CASTLE, ON THE RIVER DEE (LEFT) AND THE EDINBURGH SKYLINE AT NIGHT

THE HILL HOUSE, HELENSBURGH, ONE OF THE ARCHITECT CHARLES RENNIE MACKINTOSH'S MASTERWORKS. ADAPTING SCOTTISH BUILDING TRADITIONS, MACKINTOSH INSERTED A ROUND TOWER IN THE INNER ANGLE (AS IN MANY OLDER TOWER HOUSES) AND GAVE THE HOUSE A HARLED (ROUGH-CAST) EXTERIOR. THE INTERIOR IS ONE OF MACKINTOSH'S GREAT ACHIEVEMENTS AS A DESIGNER

SCOTLAND'S ARCHITECTURE IS ONE OF HER GLORIES. ITS HISTORY STRETCHES FROM THE BRONZE AGE, THROUGH ROMANTICALLY RUINED ABBEYS AND SPECTACULAR CASTLES, TO GEORGIAN ELEGANCE AND THE PIONEERING MODERNISM OF CHARLES RENNIE MACKINTOSH.

PREHISTORIC PLACES

SCOTLAND IS EXCEPTIONALLY RICH IN PREHISTORIC REMAINS, MANY OF THEM STILL SPECTACULARLY VISIBLE. AS IN MANY CULTURES, IMMENSE LABOUR WAS EXPENDED BY THE PREHISTORIC INHABITANTS ON RITUAL AND FUNERARY MONUMENTS, BUT STRIKING EXAMPLES ALSO SURVIVE OF PERMANENT DWELLINGS AND ELABORATELY CONSTRUCTED DEFENSIVE WORKS.

ISLAND BROCH. THIS TOWER STANDS ON THE LITTLE ISLAND OF MOUSA IN THE SHETLANDS. AT 13 METRES, IT IS THE HIGHEST AND BEST-PRESERVED OF THE BROCHS, PREHISTORIC DRYSTONE STRUCTURES THAT ARE FOUND ALL OVER THE NORTH AND WEST, BUILT TO THE SAME DESIGN AS DEFENCES AGAINST SOME NOW-UNKNOWN ENEMIES.

Some of the oldest sites are in the remotest places, on the Western and Northern Isles. Of the chambered cairns – stone-covered family graves, in use from Neolithic times – the most splendid is at Maes Howe on Orkney, with its huge blocks of beautifully fitted drystone masonry. Orkney boasts an even rarer monument in the Stone Age village at Skara Brae, beside what was then a freshwater loch offering an ample staple diet of shellfish. This village consists of ten dry-stone houses linked by covered passages, representing the remains of a settlement that existed from about 3000 BC to 2500, when it was engulfed, and preserved, by a sandstorm. Because of the lack of trees on Orkney, stone was used for the houses, for built-in cupboards, and for items of furniture such as bunks and a shelved 'dresser'; a central kerbed hearth and storage tanks in the floor provide further evidence of the ancient Orcadians' sophisticated home-making skills. Other monuments from the Neolithic and Bronze Ages were used for purposes that we can only guess at. The labour involved in raising stone circles, single or paired standing stones, and henges (concentric earthworks, with or without standing stones) makes it likely that they had a ritual or symbolic significance, possibly linking astronomical observations with events in the agricultural year; but the evidence is too fragmentary to admit of certainty.

The west coast of the Isle of Lewis has a concentration of Bronze Age sites that suggests it was once a major cult centre; the finest, at Callanish, features 'avenues' of stones from all four points of the compass leading to a thirteen-stone circle surrounding a single tall monolith. Many 'ritual' sites were occupied for up to three thousand years, doubtless modifying or completely changing their functions; the best-known example in Scotland is on Cairnpapple Hill, near Torphichen in West Lothian. The first substantial evidence of war and

insecurity dates from the 1st millennium BC, from which a variety of large defensive structures have survived. It has often been proposed that these resulted from Celtic invasions of Scotland, but such events have never been conclusively shown to have taken place, and the identities of both the defenders and their potential attackers remain unknown. The earliest structures were hill forts – that is, hilltop settlements protected by one or more rings of palisaded earth ramparts or drystone walls, surrounded by one or more ditches; two hills near Brechin, the Caterthuns, feature late, highly elaborate fortifications of this type.

Even more mysterious are the hundreds of forts and towers known as duns and brochs. Most duns are circular drystone structures, low and small enough to suggest that they may have served as refuges for single families, their very thick walls withstanding attack from passing raiders. Brochs were bigger and more castle-like, their double walls holding chambers and a spiral staircase giving access to the top. Duns appear to have been built earlier and to have continued to be built for longer, whereas all the known brochs have been dated to the 1st century BC or 1st century AD. Duns are found on the west coast and in the Hebrides, brochs in the west, the Hebrides and the north as far as the Shetlands (the best-preserved example is at Mousa on Shetland). The geographical overlap suggests, but does not prove, that brochs were developed from duns; why the Atlantic coast should have needed such protection is another so-far-unanswered question.

Apart from the remains of the Antonine Wall constructed by the Romans, monumental evidence is relatively sparse for later centuries, consisting mainly of standing stones and cross-slabs engraved with Pictish symbols, and Christian crosses and gravestones. Both of course belong to history, rather than prehistory, despite the centuries-long paucity of documentation which ended only when Scotland entered the feudal age.

A HOUSE OF STONE AT SKARA BRAE ON ORKNEY. THANKS TO THE ABSENCE OF TREES ON THE ISLAND, WHICH COMPELLED THE INHABITANTS TO BUILD IN STONE, THIS AND OTHER NEOLITHIC DWELLINGS HAVE SURVIVED THE MILLENNIA AND BEAR WITNESS TO THE HUMAN GENIUS FOR HOME-MAKING IN ALL SORTS OF CLIMES AND PLACES.

STANDING STONES AT CALLANISH ON THE ISLE OF LEWIS. THIS IS THE MOST INTRIGUING OF THE SURPRISINGLY NUMEROUS BRONZE AGE SITES ON THE ISLAND (WHICH ACTUALLY COMPRISES LEWIS AND HARRIS); 'AVENUES' OF STONES RUN FROM ALL FOUR POINTS OF THE COMPASS TO A THIRTEEN-STONE CIRCLE SURROUNDING A SINGLE TALL MONOLITH.

CHURCH AND CASTLE

THE ROMAN PRESENCE IN BRITAIN LED TO SCOTLAND'S FIRST CONTACT WITH CHRISTIANITY IN 397, WHEN ST NINIAN BEGAN HIS MISSION IN THE SOUTH-WEST. THE FOUNDATIONS OF THE FIRST CHURCH HE BUILT, AT WHITHORN, PROBABLY LIE UNDER THE EAST END OF THE PRESENT, RUINOUS PRIORY CRYPT, WHICH WAS A GREAT PILGRIMAGE CENTRE DURING THE MIDDLE AGES.

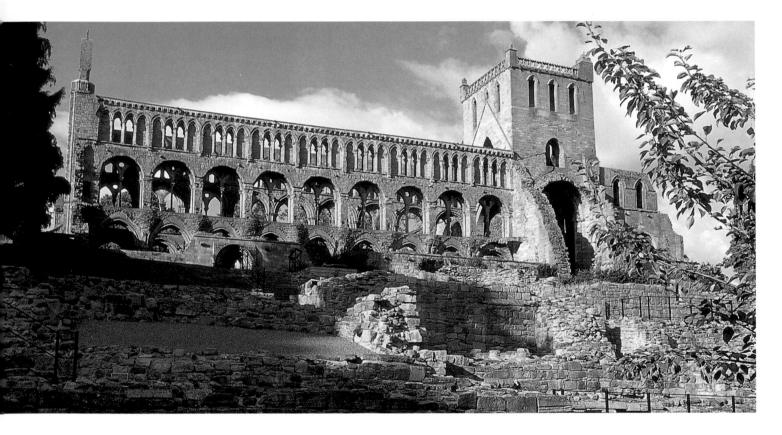

JEDBURGH ABBEY, SMALLER BUT BETTER-PRESERVED THAN KELSO AND MELROSE, THE OTHER GREAT RUINED MEDIEVAL ABBEYS OF THE BORDERS; IT WAS FOUNDED BY KING DAVID I IN 1130. THE PHOTOGRAPH SHOWS JEDBURGH'S SPLENDID ARCADING, TRANSITIONAL BETWEEN THE ROMANESQUE AND GOTHIC STYLES, AND THE IMPOSING 16TH-CENTURY TOWER OVER THE CROSSING.

However, the conversion of Scotland was not effected by the Roman Church but by monks of the Irish Celtic Church, sent out as missionaries by St Columba from his head-quarters on the island of Iona. Surviving early Christian buildings – oratories, chapels, cells – are small, reflecting the size of the population and the austere monastic outlook of the Celtic Church. The most striking remains are the monks' beehive dwellings, constructed with walls of overlapping, inward-inclined stones that met to form the roof area; there are examples on one of the Garvellach Islands (Argyll), at Eilach an Naoimh. These early structures were directly based on Irish buildings, which also provided models for the tall round towers at Brechin and Aber-nethy, built to watch for Viking raiders and to provide a refuge from them. The earlier of the towers, dating from AD 1000, is Brechin, originally free-standing but now built into the medieval church.

The main secular survivals from the period are the fortifications at Dunadd in Argyll, on the edge of Crinan Moss. This is believed to have been the first capital of Dalriada, the kingdom established in the 5th century by Scots who had crossed over from Ireland.

From the late 11th century, Scotland adopted the feudal and ecclesiastical institutions prevalent in continental Europe and, after 1066, in England. With them came castles, churches and monasteries on the European model. Malcolm III's wife, St Margaret, actively promoted both the Roman Church and the building style associated with it; the Chapel of St Margaret on Edinburgh Castle Rock, built before her death in 1093, is the oldest Scottish church in the Romanesque style of the 11th and 12th centuries. Romanesque is characterized by thick walls, mighty columns and round arches that were often elaborately and imaginatively carved; some modest Romanesque parish churches have survived the centuries (notably Dalmeny Kirk), but the most imposing examples of the style are St Magnus Cathedral, Kirkwall, on Orkney, the nave of Dunfermline Abbey, and parts of the ruined border abbey churches at Kelso and Jedburgh.

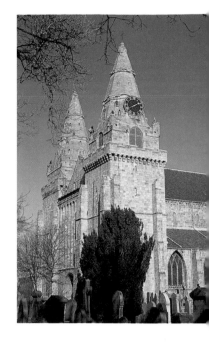

ST MACHAR'S CATHEDRAL IS THE ONLY CATHEDRAL BUILT OF GRANITE – APPROPRIATELY, SINCE IT STANDS IN THE 'GRANITE CITY', ABERDEEN. THE MASSY TOWERS ON THE WEST FRONT ARE RESPONSIBLE FOR ITS CURIOUSLY FORTRESS-LIKE APPEARANCE. ST MACHAR'S ALSO HAS A CELEBRATED HERALDIC CEILING FILLED WITH EUROPEAN AND SCOTTISH COATS OF ARMS.

The 12th-century transformation of Scotland into a feudal kingdom was symbolized by the erection of castles from which feudal lords were able to dominate their lands and the peasants who dwelt on them. Initially the castles were of the motte-and-bailey type, consisting of a palisaded timber tower on a mound (the motte), linked to a palisaded area below it (the bailey or courtyard) containing other buildings, retainers, craftsmen and so on; motte and bailey were further protected by a surrounding ditch. These structures have not survived, but in some cases the timber was subsequently replaced by stone without altering the basic layout, and Duffus and Urquhart Castles provide examples of this.

The Scots have never built massive, free-standing keeps like those of post-Conquest England (for example, Rochester Castle), probably because, by the time they possessed the resources to do so, the latest military technology favoured a very different scheme

ROSLIN CHAPEL IS IN FACT AN UNFINISHED COLLEGIATE CHURCH, DEDICATED TO ST MICHAEL AND BEGUN IN 1447; IT STANDS IN THE VILLAGE OF ROSLIN, NOT FAR FROM PENICUIK. ITS OUTSTANDING FEATURE IS THE RIOTOUS PROFUSENESS OF THE CARVING ON THE STONE SURFACES OF THE INTERIOR, MINGLING ALLEGORICAL, RELIGIOUS AND DECORATIVE DESIGNS.

of fortification. This was the castle of enceinte, in which the main defensive role was entrusted to a strong surrounding curtain wall, usually more or less quadrangular; within it, the bailey contained a hall, workshops and other structures, most of them built up against the wall. The most ambitious type of castle of enceinte was strengthened by wall-towers, mostly set into the angles, and a huge, twin-towered gatehouse that controlled the entrance and served as a defence of last resort that could be sealed off, keep-like, from the rest of the castle. Rothesay, on the Isle of Bute, is an early (12th-century) example, unusual because of its circular plan. Celebrated 13th-century examples include the large, ruinous but impressive castles of Balvenie, Kildrummy and Bothwell, and the uniquely triangular Caerlaverock Castle, near Dumfries.

There was more castle-destroying than castle-building during the 14th century Wars of Independence. Edinburgh Castle, for example, was an English stronghold, demolished after its capture by supporters of Robert Bruce; by contrast, Stirling Castle survived, despite changing hands more than once, but its timbers and earthworks were later replaced by buildings in stone, so that neither of these famous, magnificently sited structures in fact contains much medieval material.

After the wars ended, murderous baronial infighting prompted the building of such late-14th-century castles as the Stewart stronghold of Doune and the Red Douglas fortress, Tantallon, spectacularly located on a clifftop looking out over the North Sea.

A TRIANGULAR CASTLE. CAERLAVEROCK, NEAR DUMFRIES, ORIGINATED IN THE 13TH CENTURY BUT WAS SEVERAL TIMES DAMAGED AND REBUILT OVER THE FOLLOWING FOUR HUNDRED YEARS WHILE RETAINING ITS STRIKINGLY UNUSUAL FORM, WITH CURTAIN WALLS ON THREE SIDES, A TOWER AT EACH OF TWO ANGLES, AND A DOUBLE-TOWERED GATEWAY, SURROUNDED BY A MOAT.

But the chronic insecurity of late-medieval Scottish life is most graphically illustrated by the large numbers of a new type of fortified residence, built from the 14th century right through to the early 17th. The tower house was like a smaller version of the keep, a rectangular block with thick walls that would resist most efforts to knock them through or down. They were not designed to withstand a long siege, but to protect the local laird and his family during a raid until help arrived or the raiders moved on. The hall and living quarters were in the upper storeys, above a windowless ground floor filled with provisions; the entrance was on the first floor, reached by steps or a ladder which could be removed when danger threatened. The tower house was often given a little extra protection by a curtain wall that created a barmkin, or courtyard, for the house and its outbuildings; but the tower house was the vital component, allowing the inhabitants to hold out even when taken by surprise or hopelessly outnumbered.

The effectiveness of the tower house is demonstrated by the fact that hundreds still survive. An early example is the suitably grim Threave Castle, one of the border strongholds of the Black Douglases, which stands on an island in the River Dee. By the 15th century, some tower houses were being enlarged or built on new plans that afforded the residents more spacious accommodation. Adding an extra tower at an angle created the L-plan, as at Craigmillar Castle; adding two towers, one at each end of two diagonally opposite corners, created the Z-plan found, for example, at Claypotts. As time went on, comfort and ornament became increasingly important, leading to enlargements of the safe upper storeys; as a result, a tower house such as the early 17th-century Craigievar Castle is more like a fairy-tale residence than a relative of bold, bad, baronial Threave.

CRAIGIEVAR CASTLE, PERHAPS THE MOST SPECTACULAR EXAMPLE OF THE SCOTTISH TASTE FOR BUILDING TALL; THE CHARM OF THIS TOWER HOUSE IS ACCENTUATED BY THE PINK HARLING AND CLUSTER OF TURRETS ON ITS SKYLINE. IT WAS PUT UP IN 1620-26 BY THE MERCHANT WILLIAM FORBES, KNOWN AS 'DANZIG WILLIE' BECAUSE OF HIS BALTIC TRADING CONNECTIONS.

Ecclesiastical architecture in Scotland developed along lines laid down on the Continent, making the transition from Romanesque to the Gothic style with its characteristic pointed arches and a general lightness made possible by engineering innovations. As a result of wars and religious struggles, many of the finest buildings are now magnificent ruins, though still with many interesting architectural as well as picturesque features; among the best known are the great Cistercian abbeys of Jedburgh, Dryburgh and Melrose in border territory, Arbroath Abbey and Holyrood Abbey in Edinburgh. Other buildings have been added to over the centuries, or over-thoroughly restored, but Gothic is well represented in Glasgow Cathedral, St Giles, Edinburgh, and St Marchant's, Aberdeen, while Roslin Chapel is most un-Scottish in the spirit of ornamental excess in which the late Gothic (Decorated) style is interpreted, so that even the smallest surface is covered with a mass of intricate carving.

HOUSES AND PALACES

SCOTLAND ENJOYED A LONG PERIOD OF PEACE AND REL-
ATIVE GOOD ORDER DURING THE LATE 16TH AND EARLY
17TH CENTURIES. THIS ENCOURAGED BUILDING, AND IN
PARTICULAR BUILDING FOR COMFORT RATHER THAN
SECURITY, BY AN UPPER CLASS WHOSE WEALTH HAD
BEEN INCREASED BY THE ACQUISITION OF CHURCH
LANDS DURING THE REFORMATION.

One symptom of this was the expansion of the upper storeys of
tower houses to provide extra accommodation; but building was no
longer inevitably upwards, and many lairds enlarged the halls of their
castles or added residential ranges to existing structures, as at Drum
Castle near Aberdeen. In effect, wealthy Scots turned from fortress- to
mansion-building, and the tower began to be replaced by, or transformed into, a country house.

A ROYAL PALACE. FALKLAND PALACE WAS BUILT BY
KINGS JAMES IV AND JAMES V IN THE FIRST HALF OF
THE 16TH CENTURY, WHEN RENAISSANCE IDEAS WERE
BEGINNING TO INFLUENCE SCOTTISH ARCHITECTURE.
THE BULKY TWIN-TOWERED GATEHOUSE IS STILL IN THE
TRADITION OF DEFENSIVE BUILDING, THE TOWERS
SERVING TO PROTECT THE ENTRANCE FROM AN ASSAULT.

There was also much new royal building.
Linlithgow Palace was almost continuously
enlarged from the 15th century onwards.
Late in the century the Great Hall was added
to Stirling Castle, and in the 1540s James V
built the palace there. Both Stirling and Falkland Palace display elements of the
Renaissance style, with its symmetrical plans,
round arches, columns and colonnades and
pediments; originating in Italy, it may have
been introduced to Scotland by the French
craftsmen who came to the country after
James married Mary of Guise.

The Renaissance style ultimately derived
from the architecture of ancient ('classical')
Greece and Rome, which in various modified
forms (Baroque, Palladian, Neo-Classical)
provided the main model for European buildings right down to the 19th century. But in
Scotland the royal experiments found few
imitators until the late 17th century, though
Renaissance ornamental details were often
incorporated in new or enlarged buildings.
The grand residence remained a mixture of
styles, often very effective in their accumu-
lated elements, as at such well-known places
as Lennoxlove and Traquair House.

Towns also expanded in the 16th century,
when their prosperity and sense of security
were asserted by the replacement of wooden
buildings (easily destroyed but also easily

PROVOST SKENE'S HOUSE IN ABERDEEN. THIS STURDY, TURRETED TOWN HOUSE DATES BACK TO THE 16TH CENTURY, ALTHOUGH IT IS NAMED AFTER THE MAYOR, PROVOST SKENE, WHO OWNED IT FROM 1669. ITS LONG GALLERY HAS A PAINTED CEILING WITH RELIGIOUS SUBJECTS, EXCEPTIONAL IN ESCAPING THE ATTENTIONS OF PROTESTANT ICONOCLASTS.

rebuilt) by stone, which was more prestigious and less combustible. Town houses were typically two-story structures with harled walls (that is, covered with a rough-cast rendering), small windows, crowstepped gables which often faced the street, and very big 'lums' (chimneys). Only a few town houses from before 1600 survive, the best-known being two Edinburgh dwellings, 'John Knox's House' in the High Street and Huntly House in the Canongate, and the even older (1471) Provand's Lordship in Glasgow; of 17th-century buildings, Gladstone's Land in Edinburgh's Lawnmarket is a particularly fine example of a merchant's house and emporium. The typical layout of the town, described earlier, remained unaffected by the transition to stone, but as urban life became more attractive to noblemen, they built town mansions for themselves. One such (despite its name) is Culross Palace, part of which dates back to 1597; while Argyll's Lodging at Stirling and Acheson House, Edinburgh, are only a little later in date. On a much grander scale, George Heriot's Hospital (also known as George Heriot's School) was built from 1627 at Lauriston, then outside Edinburgh, by the royal master mason William Wallace, the first Scottish architect to be known by name. Heriot's, founded as a free school for fatherless boys, is in effect a quadrangular Renaissance palace

GEORGE HERIOT'S HOSPITAL IN EDINBURGH: A MID-19TH-CENTURY ENGRAVING SHOWING THE WEST AND NORTH SIDES OF THE COURTYARD. IT IS BUILT IN AN ORNATE, MODIFIED VERSION OF THE RENAISSANCE STYLE, WITH CUPOLAS, TOWERS, TURRETS, TRACERY AND PEDIMENTED WINDOWS. HERIOT WAS AN EDINBURGH BANKER WHO LEFT MONEY TO FOUND THE HOSPITAL.

INVERARAY CASTLE, BUILT FOR THE DUKES OF ARGYLL, WAS A MANSION PUT UP TO REPLACE AN OLDER TOWER HOUSE. WHEN VICTORIAN 'BARONIAL' BEGAN TO REPLACE REAL WITH MOCK-DEFENSIVE STRUCTURES, IT WAS TURNED INTO A 'CASTLE' BY THE ADDITION OF THE CONE-TOPPED TOWERS AND THE 'BATTLEMENTS' WHICH CURIOUSLY DOUBLE AS DORMER WINDOWS.

built round a courtyard. Despite the inclusion of Scottish, Flemish and English elements, it is the first Scottish building to go beyond a superficial use of Renaissance ornament.

Wallace's work at Heriot's and Winton House was limited in its immediate influence. The wars and upheavals of the mid-17th century inhibited ambitious building, and the first entirely coherent classical schemes were only introduced to Scotland some years after the restoration of the king in 1660. This was the achievement of the widely travelled Sir William Bruce. Appointed Surveyor-General of the King's Works in Scotland, Bruce employed his knowledge of continental models to reconstruct the partly-destroyed royal palace of Holyroodhouse, Edinburgh, which assumed essentially its present-day appearance in the 1670s. He was even more widely active and influential as an adviser to mansion-building aristocrats than as a practising architect; his surviving masterpiece is Kinross House, set in superb formal gardens on the edge of Loch Leven.

One of Bruce's late projects was Hopetoun House (West Lothian), but his design was not completely realized and the mansion was greatly enlarged following the elevation of its owner, Sir Charles Hope, to an earldom. The architect was Bruce's pupil, William Adam, who had toured England and absorbed the current style, a form of classicism that was at once lighter and grander than Bruce's. Hopetoun, with its central block linked to wings by sweeping colonnades, is reminiscent of palatial country mansions by Vanbrugh, the architect of Blenheim and Castle Howard.

The replacement of the formal garden by a 'natural' landscaped garden was also a sign of the times. In Hopetoun House and his other works, William Adam brought Scottish architecture close to English fashions. His fame has been eclipsed by that of his son, Robert Adam, an architect of international influence who studied Roman remains and subsequently popularized a more restrained and correct Neo-Classical style. His most striking achievements were in the treatment of interiors, which he revolutionized by widening the current classical vocabulary and creating comprehensive decorative schemes for which he designed every detail including the furniture.

Most of Adam's career was spent in England, where he created masterpieces such as Kedleston Hall, Syon House, Osterley Park and Kenwood, all from the 1750s and '60s. He might have left little of note in his native land if his ambitious Adelphi scheme in London had not proved a financial disaster. The blow to his reputation was severe, and largely as a result he worked mainly in Scotland from the mid-1770s to his death in 1792. He was very active in Edinburgh, where the City Chambers and some individual houses and university buildings by him survive; but his best-known works in the capital are the grandly restrained Register House and the supremely elegant Charlotte Square. Elsewhere, he built Trades House in Glasgow and, in a very different vein, Culzean and Seton Castles, early Scottish examples of the battlemented 'Gothic' mansion, playfully masquerading as a medieval fortress.

Town planning was, for all practical purposes, an invention of the 18th century, reflecting both the affluence and the rationality of the age. But the motive was not always coolly rational: the 3rd Duke of Argyll was so irritated by the common people's houses within sight of his castle that in 1744 he rebuilt the town, Inverary, on a more comfortably distant site, beside Loch Fyne. By contrast, fishing towns such as Ullapool were founded in the late 18th century in an attempt to revive the economy of the north; and planned additions to Aberdeen and other cities reflected Scotland's growing urban prosperity and population. Whether planned or not, Georgian houses became one of the great charms of Scottish towns and villages. But there was nothing to match the scale of the New Town laid out in Edinburgh, where Adam's contributions to the cityscape, though important, were only one element in its great 18th-century transformation from 'Auld Reekie' to 'the Athens of the North'.

AN ADAM INTERIOR AT CULZEAN CASTLE. CULZEAN WAS AN EXAMPLE OF A 'GOTHICK' BUILDING, PUT UP IN A PLAYFUL 18TH-CENTURY SPIRIT OF MOCK-MEDIEVALISM THAT TOOK A MORE SERIOUS TURN IN VICTORIAN TIMES. HOWEVER, IN DESIGNING THE INTERIOR, THE ARCHITECT OF CULZEAN, ROBERT ADAM, REVERTED TO HIS SUPREMELY ELEGANT NEO-CLASSICAL STYLE.

OLD TOWN, NEW TOWN

EDINBURGH HAS BEEN THE ACKNOWLEDGED CAPITAL OF SCOTLAND SINCE THE 15TH CENTURY, AND WAS THE COUNTRY'S MOST POPULOUS AND PROSPEROUS CITY UNTIL THE INDUSTRIAL REVOLUTION LED TO THE HEADLONG GROWTH OF GLASGOW. SOME PART OF THE HILLY SITE HAS BEEN OCCUPIED BY HUMAN BEINGS SINCE VERY EARLY TIMES, INITIALLY BECAUSE OF THE DEFENSIVE SECURITY OFFERED BY CASTLE ROCK, A CLIFF WITH THREE SHEER SIDES, APPROACHABLE ONLY ALONG THE RIDGE (NOW THE ROYAL MILE) THAT SLOPES AWAY FROM IT TOWARDS THE EAST.

Castle Rock, like Arthur's Seat and other surrounding hilltops, was probably fortified by the 1st millennium BC; but when the Romans occupied the area they set up naval supply bases on the Forth to the west and east, at Cramond and Inveresk. Edinburgh makes its first significant appearance in history as a stronghold on Castle Rock known as Din Eidyn. Captured early in the 7th century by the Angles, it was a frontier post until Malcolm II brought the Lothian region under Scots control in 1018. Non-military settlement along the ridge probably began at some time after this, and it can be inferred from surviving documents that by 1124 Edinburgh was a royal burgh. Canongate, further down the ridge, became a burgh in 1128, with Holyrood Abbey at its base; the guesthouse of the abbey developed into the splendid royal Palace of Holyroodhouse. Though effectively a suburb of Edinburgh, the Canongate remained technically independent of the city until the 19th century.

ADVOCATE'S CLOSE, JUST OFF THE HIGH STREET (ROYAL MILE), IN THE MID-19TH CENTURY; PAINTING BY WILLIAM SIMPSON. THIS VERTIGINOUS PICTURE CAPTURES THE DISTINCTIVE QUALITY OF THE OLD TOWN, WITH ITS SIX-STOREY TENEMENTS AND RESTRICTED OPEN SPACES. LIKE OTHER ONCE RUN-DOWN SITES, A RENOVATED ADVOCATE'S CLOSE NOW ATTRACTS MANY VISITORS.

Despite vicissitudes in the wars against England, Edinburgh emerged from the Middle Ages as the most important Scottish burgh, with a substantial Lothian hinterland and a thriving trade with the Low Countries and the Baltic through the port of Leith, three kilometres away on the shores of the Forth. Suburbs developed to the south of the ridge in the Cowgate and the Grassmarket, and in the mid-15th century the King's Wall was thrown up to protect these southern approaches. The ravine to the north was made more formidable by the creation of an artificial lake, the Nor' Loch (now Princes Street Gardens). After the disaster at Flodden, the King's Wall was hastily replaced by a higher, stronger structure, the Flodden Wall.

The Wall failed to prevent the last of the city's serious military misfortunes. In 1544 it was taken, and much of it burned, by an English expeditionary force. Recovery was swift,

GLADSTONE'S LAND IS A 17TH-CENTURY MERCHANT'S HOUSE IN EDINBURGH'S LAWNMARKET WITH AN ARCADED GROUND FLOOR, AN OUTSIDE STAIRCASE, AND TWO SMALL CROW-STEPPED GABLES AT THE TOP OF ITS SIX STOREYS; THE INTERIOR ALSO CONTAINS INTERESTING FEATURES. A 'LAND' IS A BUILDING RENTED TO A DIFFERENT TENANT ON EACH FLOOR.

and the disaster probably speeded up the transition from using wood to building in stone, although a number of 17th-century ordinances make it clear that timber and thatch had continued to be used. The most important effect of the Flodden Wall was to inhibit building to the south, so that the expanding population was housed in ever-taller tenements that became a distinctive feature of the city.

Edinburgh lost some of its lustre after 1603, when king and court moved to London. But its primacy in Scotland remained unchallenged throughout the upheavals of the 17th century, and it was the natural centre for the new financial and commercial institutions that developed towards the end of the period. Although small by international standards (in 1700 the population was still only about 20,000), 18th-century Edinburgh became the heart of the Scottish Enlightenment, counting many of the greatest intellects of the age among its inhabitants.

Appropriately, this flowering coincided with the decisive expansion of the city. Known as 'Auld Reekie' on account of its thousands of smoking chimneys, Edinburgh remained a dirty, cramped and unsafe place with crumbling tenements and dark, insanitary closes. After many delays, the city council secured permission to expand the

HOLYROODHOUSE IS STILL THE OFFICIAL RESIDENCE OF THE MONARCH IN SCOTLAND, BUT ITS GREAT DAYS ENDED WHEN JAMES VI BECAME KING OF ENGLAND AND THE COURT MOVED SOUTH. THE MOST DRAMATIC EPISODE IN ITS HISTORY WAS THE MURDER OF DAVID RIZZIO, THE ITALIAN SECRETARY OF MARY, QUEEN OF SCOTS, BY NOBLES IN LEAGUE WITH HER HUSBAND.

boundaries and in 1766 held a competition to find the most suitable design for a new development on the other side of the Nor' Loch. The winner was twenty-two-year old James Craig, who proposed a set of classical terraces in a regular grid-plan, consisting of three parallel main thoroughfares (Princes, George and Queen Streets) terminating at each end with a square (St Andrew's and Charlotte Square). This became known as the New Town, extended over subsequent decades to some 300 hectares, making it the largest and most spectacular of all Georgian city developments. Meanwhile a North Bridge was begun to link the Old and New Towns, the Flodden Wall was dismantled to allow the Old Town to expand to the south, and the Nor' Loch (by this time a notorious cesspool) was drained in stages, eventually making it possible to fill the ravine with Princes Street Gardens and the Mound.

Other familiar features were established in the 1840s, when the 55-metre-high Scott Monument was erected on Princes Street and the central railway station, Waverley (another tribute to Scott), was built. Edinburgh was relatively little affected by the Industrial Revolution, and much of its Victorian building was devoted to business rather than manufacturing premises; the New Town remained largely intact apart from Princes Street, which was made over as the main shopping thoroughfare and, as such, has continued to attract the attentions of the developer. Victorian renovation of the Old Town was an unquestionable advance, although its 'Auld Reekie' aspect only disappeared for good in recent times with the enforcement of the Clean Air Acts. Spared during the Second World War, Edinburgh entered the post-war period as a gem of a city with a promising future.

Occupied by English and French garrisons and the Highland following of Bonnie Prince Charlie, Edinburgh has played a prominent part in Scottish history. It has also witnessed many dark deeds. In Edinburgh Castle, at the Black Dinner of 1440, the young Douglas brothers were dragged from the presence of the even younger James II and executed. Faction-fights were common, including the High Street encounter in 1520 between the Douglases and the Hamiltons, known as 'Cleanse-the-Causeway' from the bloody remains left for the citizenry to

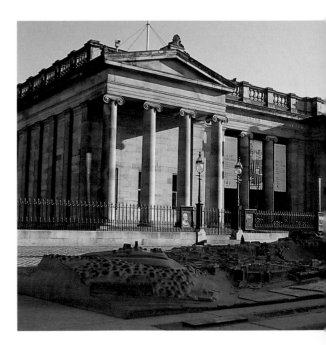

THE NATIONAL GALLERY OF SCOTLAND IS PART OF EDINBURGH'S LARGE NEO-CLASSICAL HERITAGE, CREATING A VERY DIFFERENT EFFECT FROM THAT OF THE OLD TOWN TENEMENTS. DESIGNED BY WILLIAM PLAYFAIR AND BUILT IN THE EARLY 1850S, THE GALLERY POSSESSES AN OUTSTANDING COLLECTION OF OLD MASTERS AND HOSTS MAJOR EXHIBITIONS DURING THE EDINBURGH FESTIVAL.

A PUBLIC HANGING. THE OCCASION IS THE EXECUTION OF THE MURDERER WILLIAM BURKE, WHOSE VICTIMS WERE SOLD TO THE ANATOMIST ROBERT KNOX; BURKE WAS CONVICTED ON THE BASIS OF EVIDENCE GIVEN BY HIS PARTNER IN CRIME, WILLIAM HARE, WHO TURNED KING'S EVIDENCE. IN THE BACKGROUND, ST GILES CATHEDRAL OVERLOOKS THE SCENE.

remove. The Reformation brought popular participation in religious upheavals, most notably in 1637, when a woman named Jenny Geddes is said to have flung a stool at the Dean, leading to mass protests against the introduction of the English prayer-book and the signing of the National Covenant in Greyfriars' Kirk. The people of Edinburgh remained unruly into the 18th century, rioting in vain against their parliament's acceptance of union with England, and in 1736 forcibly removing from custody and hanging John Porteous, the captain of the town guard, when it seemed possible that he would escape punishment for having shot down protesting citizens.

The later history of the city was less tumultuous, though two criminal cases have become part of the city's folklore. William Brodie was the respectable head of a cabinetmaking workshop, deacon of his guild and a town councillor. But in 1787 a man detained after a bungled burglary turned informer and named Brodie as the leader of his gang in their nocturnal excursions. Brodie fled abroad but was captured in Amsterdam, brought back to Edinburgh and hanged. The double life of 'Deacon Brodie', and the absence of any known motive for his criminal activities, made him a fascinating figure – to, among others, Robert Louis Stevenson, who may have derived some of his inspiration for the dual characters of Dr Jekyll and Mr Hyde from the deacon.

The other memorable case was that of the murderers Burke and Hare, two Irish workmen who exploited the shortage of cadavers needed for dissection in anatomy classes. One illicit source of supplies was the 'resurrectionist' who surreptitiously dug up corpses and sold them; but Burke and Hare adopted a less laborious approach, simply murdering vagrants whom no one would miss. Eventually they were arrested and, to secure a conviction, Hare was allowed to turn King's Evidence, going free in return for incriminating his accomplice; Burke was duly hanged in January 1829. Perhaps the most intriguing aspect of the case was the ambiguous role played by the anatomy lecturer Robert Knox, who was guileless or callous enough to accept the sixteen corpses supplied by the murderers without asking any awkward questions.

VICTORIAN HEYDAY

THE 19TH CENTURY WAS ONE OF THE GREAT ERAS OF BUILDING, IN QUANTITY IF NOT ALWAYS IN QUALITY. AS THE PACE OF THE INDUSTRIAL REVOLUTION QUICKENED, MORE NEW OR TECHNOLOGICALLY REMODELLED STRUCTURES WERE BUILT, AMONG THEM BRIDGES, FACTORIES, WAREHOUSES AND RAILWAY STATIONS.

VICTORIAN NEO-GOTHIC ON THE HEROIC SCALE: GLASGOW UNIVERSITY, SPREAD OUT ON GILMOREHILL, WITH ITS 100-METRE TOWER DOMINATING THE SKYLINE. WHEN THE ANCIENT UNIVERSITY HAD TO MOVE FROM THE HIGH STREET, THE NEW BUILDING ON THE HILL WAS DESIGNED BY THE PROLIFIC SIR GEORGE GILBERT SCOTT AND BUILT BETWEEN 1874 AND 1891.

Materials such as iron and steel played a large part in Victorian engineering and were sometimes also used for the booming commercial buildings that were transforming most city centres. Glasgow in particular acquired shops, warehouses, railway termini and a variety of fine municipal buildings, becoming a great, if grimy, Victorian city, all too much of which was demolished, instead of being renovated, in the delirium of 're-development' during the 1960s.

By contrast with their engineering feats, the Victorians proved singularly uninventive when confronted with buildings that they regarded as 'architecture' rather than merely functional structures. In designing suburban villas, country houses, tenements, banks, libraries and churches, architects looked to the past for styles in which to clothe the buildings. This trend, known as historicism, intensified in the course of the century, as more and more styles and sub-styles were taken up in a quest for originality of a sort, and leading architects rang the changes between Neo-Classical, Neo-Gothic, French Renaissance, Venetian Gothic, and so on. At the same time, up-to-date skills were applied where it mattered: Jacobean or Renaissance country houses were equipped with billiard rooms and other necessaries, and great ingenuity was devoted to laying out segregated servants' quarters whose inhabitants should be as nearly invisible as possible. Similarly, behind the Venetian Gothic façade of the Royal Scottish Museum in Edinburgh lay a splendid, airy main hall with slender cast-iron columns and a light-maximizing glass and timber roof.

Building in the classical tradition carried on all through the 19th century, but perhaps the most interesting development was the

ABBOTSFORD, THE STATELY HOME CREATED BY SIR WALTER SCOTT, IS ACTUALLY PRE-VICTORIAN, DATING FROM THE 1810S. BUT IT PROVIDED A MODEL FOR MUCH LATER SCOTTISH BUILDING IN ITS ECLECTIC HISTORICISM AND HIGH-TOWERED BARONIAL AIR. SCOTT'S RECKLESS EXPENDITURE ON ABBOTSFORD WAS A FACTOR IN THE FINANCIAL CATASTROPHE THAT OVERTOOK HIM.

Greek Revival during the first half of the period. Ancient Greek architectural styles predated those of Rome and were generally simpler and more severe (especially the earliest style or Order, the Doric). A more scholarly appreciation of Greek architecture, and no doubt a reaction against Adam opulence, culminated in the Revival, which had an international influence. In Scotland it had a significant effect on the character of Edinburgh, where William Henry Playfair and Thomas Hamilton were very active. Playfair designed extensions to the New Town, monuments on Calton Hill that have become well-known landmarks, and the Royal Scottish Academy (1826) and National Gallery of Scotland (1854) on the Mound; Hamilton's work included the Royal High School (1829), a Doric building directly based on the Athenian Temple of Theseus. The Greek Revival style lasted longer in Glasgow and produced its greatest exponent in Alexander 'Greek' Thomson, designer of the impressively massy Great Western Terrace (1869). Despite his sobriquet, Thomson skilfully inserted Egyptian features into some of his designs, including the celebrated St Vincent Street Free Church (1859) and Egyptian Hall (1871).

The most important of the other revivals was Gothic. Used in the 18th century for the almost frivolous medievalizing of secular buildings, Gothic became the style of high seriousness in the Victorian era, widely applied (for example to Sir George Gilbert Scott's Glasgow University) and virtually mandatory for the many churches built during the period. It was also the medium through which patriotic reverence was expressed, in the towering Scott Monument on Edinburgh's Princes Street and the actual tower of the Wallace Monument at Stirling.

One specifically Scottish revival enjoyed enormous popularity. 'Scottish Baronial' was based on the battlements, irregular skylines, cone-topped towers and turrets, crowstepped gables and other features of fortified buildings in earlier centuries. Popularized by Sir Walter Scott's mansion, Abbotsford (1822), it received royal approval with the building of Balmoral in 1852–4 and was adopted with greater or lesser degrees of fantasy for everything from castellated mansions and resort hotels to villas and city tenements.

LIGHT, MODERN AND AIRY, THE BURRELL GALLERY ON THE POLLOCK ESTATE OUTSIDE GLASGOW IS A MASTERPIECE OF CONTEMPORARY SCOTTISH ARCHITECTURE, ADMIRED NOT ONLY BY SPECIALISTS BUT BY VISITORS TO THE GREAT ART COLLECTION LEFT TO GLASGOW BY WILLIAM BURRELL. THE BUILDING WAS DESIGNED BY BARRY GASSON AND OPENED IN 1983.

CHARLES RENNIE MACKINTOSH

LATE 19TH-CENTURY SCOTLAND PRODUCED AN ARCHI-
TECT OF INTERNATIONAL STATURE IN CHARLES RENNIE
MACKINTOSH. NOW REGARDED AS ONE OF GLASGOW'S
GREATEST SONS, DURING HIS LIFETIME, MATTERS WERE
VERY DIFFERENT.

UNCONVENTIONAL BUT PRACTICAL, THE LIBRARY
OF THE GLASGOW SCHOOL OF ART IS ONE OF
MACKINTOSH'S MOST ADMIRED INTERIORS, ITS PLAIN,
DARK TIMBER PILLARS RISING FROM THE FLOOR TO THE
COFFERED CEILING, ITS CLUSTERS OF LAMPSHADES
ASTONISHINGLY MODERN IN FORM, AND ITS SET-BACK
GALLERY LINKED TO THE PILLARS BY LINES OF
DISCREETLY COLOURFUL BALUSTERS.

Mackintosh was born in Glasgow on 7 June 1868, the second of eleven children. He served a five-year apprenticeship before joining the architectural firm of Honeyman and Keppie in 1889. For years he was occupied with routine tasks, finding a creative outlet in evening classes at the Glasgow School of Art, where he became associated with Herbert MacNair and the Margaret and Frances Macdonald. As 'the Four' they exercised a certain influence in Glasgow, producing Symbolist and Art Nouveau work.

His chance came in 1896, when he won the competition to design a new Glasgow School of Art. The competition stipulated that the building must be plain and inexpensive; Mackintosh fulfilled the brief while producing a masterly structure, with the large windows appropriate to the school's function, that was free from the prevailing historicism. Although 'total' design was in fashion during the 1890s, Mackintosh was exceptional in his attention to every detail of the fittings and furnishings, which became individual objects of beauty while also being in complete harmony with their surroundings.

Some features of Mackintosh's personal idiom as a designer were his employment of large areas of white in interiors, his preference for tall verticals and grid and ladder forms, and his use of mirror glass, stained glass and mother-of-pearl. His curves and floral ornaments are so restrained that he refused to acknowledge their relationship to the undulations and swelling forms of Art Nouveau, and indeed his work was hailed on the Continent as the last word in modernism. Mackintosh and Margaret Macdonald, not long married, went to Vienna in 1900 and exhibited at the annual Secession exhibition, where Mackintosh was toasted by his Austrian colleagues as a master and mentor.

In 1902 his designs were acclaimed again at Turin, but there was no such excitement in Britain. However, Mackintosh was kept busy over the next few years, and although he was often subject to irksome constraints, he demonstrated how an architect of genius could add distinction to even the most conventional briefs, as at the *Daily Record* newspaper office (1901) and, especially, Scotland Street School (1904–6). Of his two domestic commissions outside Glasgow, the Hill House at Helensburgh (1902–4) survives, incorporating traditional Scottish features (notably a harled exterior and a round stair tower set in the inner angle of the building) without falling into baronial excess.

In the 1900s much of Mackintosh's time and energy was taken up by designs for Glasgow tea rooms to provide a temperance alternative to public houses; though not projects usually associated with great architecture and design, in Mackintosh's hands they became sumptuous pleasure palaces offering a refuge from the city streets.

In 1907–9 Mackintosh was the architect in charge of building the west wing of Glasgow School of Art. This is generally considered to be his greatest work, its soaring vertical bays of glass and stone contrived to exploit the sloping site; the library, housed in the west wing, is a major achievement of interior design. Astonishingly, none of this made any impact outside Glasgow, and other large-scale commissions eluded Mackintosh. He had been taken into partnership at Honeyman and Keppie's in 1904, but alcohol and frustration made his behaviour increasingly erratic, and the partnership was dissolved in 1913.

The Mackintoshes left Glasgow, settled briefly in Suffolk, and then, on the outbreak of the First World War, moved to Chelsea in London, where they supported themselves by designing fabrics. The remodelling of a house in Northampton (1916) showed that Mackintosh was as skilful as ever, but none of his architectural projects materialized. From 1923 he worked in the south of France as a watercolourist, dying of cancer on 11 December 1928.

Mackintosh's life ended in apparent failure and a number of his buildings were demolished. But in recent decades posterity has tried to make amends. Trademark Mackintosh motifs are everywhere in Glasgow. The Hunterian Art Gallery has recreated the interior of the Mackintoshes' own home; the House for an Art Lover, from a never-executed design, stands in Bellahouston Park; and on Sauchiehall Street a reconstructed Willow Tea Rooms is now crowded with art-lovers.

HILL HOUSE IS THE ONLY DOMESTIC COMMISSION BY MACKINTOSH THAT SURVIVES IN ITS ORIGINAL FORM AND ON ITS INTENDED SITE. THE EXTERIOR IS SHOWN ON PAGE 128. THE DRAWING ROOM (ABOVE) EXEMPLIFIES MACKINTOSH'S TASTE FOR TALL LINEAR FORMS AND HIS AUDACIOUS USE OF WHITE AND ABOLITION OF CLUTTER IN HIS INTERIORS.

THE WEST WING OF GLASGOW SCHOOL OF ART. MACKINTOSH'S MOST FAMOUS WORK, THE SCHOOL IS NOW MUCH-VISITED BY ADMIRERS BUT STILL FUNCTIONS AS A COLLEGE; PAINSTAKINGLY DESIGNED INTERIOR DETAILS SUCH AS DOORS AND HANDLES HAVE AN ATTRACTIVELY WELL-USED APPEARANCE, THEIR CENTURY-LONG SURVIVAL TESTIFYING TO THEIR PRACTICALITY.

CONTEMPORARY SCOTLAND

ABOVE: The tower of the Museum of Scotland extension, 1998 (left) and yachts at anchor in the harbour at Aberdeen

DUNDEE CITY SQUARE and High Street. Formerly the great centre of the jute industry, Dundee emerged in the 1990s from a period of steep industrial decline with diversified enterprises and a refurbished centre

SURVIVING THE DECLINE OF HER OLD
INDUSTRIES, SCOTLAND HAS EMERGED AS A
SOPHISTICATED PLAYER ON THE 'POST-
MODERN' SCENE, WITH A PARLIAMENT OF
HER OWN FOR THE FIRST TIME IN ALMOST 300
YEARS.

ROLLER-COASTER YEARS

SCOTLAND EMERGED FROM THE SECOND WORLD WAR WITH MIXED PROSPECTS. THE CONFLICT HAD REVIVED DEPRESSED INDUSTRIES, CREATING A HUGE DEMAND FOR SHIPS, MACHINERY AND MUNITIONS THAT GAVE EMPLOYMENT TO ALL.

But, quite apart from the effects of German bombing, problems of poverty, deprivation and poor health remained, and these were compounded by the still hopelessly inadequate state of Scottish housing, which had certainly not improved during the interwar years, when the public sector was conspicuously neglected.

Over the next few decades, vigorous government intervention made up for some past shortcomings. The heavy industries managed to stay in business – with increasing difficulty – and there was a marked improvement in social conditions. Near-full employment was sustained, the establishment of the Welfare State brought greater security and better public health through the National Health Service, and energetic house-building and slum clearance schemes were put in hand. Unfortunately, although squalid tenements disappeared from city centres and previously notorious black spots such as the Gorbals, the buildings that replaced them were not always sound, and the former slum-dwellers were generally settled on edge-of-the-town estates with few amenities and few prospects of generating jobs if the good times came to an end.

Progress continued to be made in the 1960s and '70s, with Scots benefiting from the affluence that had become general in the western world. Standards of living went on rising despite the fact that shipping, steel and other core industries were finding it nearly impossible to match the prices charged by their foreign competitors; the causes were many, but certainly included the difficulties faced by most long-established industries (heavy investment in facilities that were becoming technically outmoded) as well as a legacy of bad labour relations from the bitter struggles of the past. But British governments were committed to maintaining regional prosperity and were acutely aware that over a third of the Scottish population was concentrated in the industrial belt that stretched across the Central Lowlands. Consequently government initiatives and subsidies played a supportive role that staved off collapse for a remarkably long time.

LEITH, ONCE A BUSY PORT, DECAYED TO THE POINT WHERE, A FEW YEARS AGO, ITS GENERAL CONDITION WAS SLUM-LIKE. NOW PART OF EDINBURGH, IT HAS BECOME HIGHLY FASHIONABLE, ITS TENEMENTS AND WAREHOUSES RENOVATED AS OFFICES AND FLATS, AND ITS QUAYS HOME TO BISTROS, WINE BARS AND SIMILARLY SOPHISTICATED DEVELOPMENTS.

A HYDRO-ELECTRIC DAM IN OPERATION AT LOCH LAGGAN. SCOTLAND'S ABUNDANCE OF WATER (THE UP-SIDE OF ITS HEAVY RAINFALL) HAS MADE HYDRO-ELECTRIC POWER ATTRACTIVE, AND IT FEATURED PROMINENTLY IN POST-WAR EFFORTS TO REGENERATE THE HIGHLAND ECONOMY. PROPOSALS FOR ITS FURTHER EXPANSION HAVE AROUSED MUCH CONTROVERSY.

Then, from 1979, Britain was ruled by a British government, led by Mrs Thatcher, which condemned state intervention and subsidies, putting the free operation of the market at the centre of its economic policies. In Scotland the removal of subsidies and support helped to ensure that the decline of the heavy industries would accelerate. Despite reassurances and optimistic forecasts, this went on through the 1980s, and the closing of the Ravenscraig steelworks in 1991 effectively marked the end of Scotland's industrial era.

Scotland, along with most of the western world, moved into an age which could be described in terms of either opportunity or insecurity, characterized by private-sector growth, higher unemployment and a widening gap between haves and have-nots. Initially disadvantaged by the relatively sluggish development of service industries, Scotland did benefit from the discovery that there were huge offshore deposits of natural gas and, above all, oil in the North Sea. The first major finds dated back to 1970, but large-scale exploitation only became highly profitable after (OPEC), the organization of the established oil-producing countries, raised prices dramatically in 1973–4. Sullom Voe on Shetland sprang from obscurity to become Britain's largest oil terminal, the largest refinery was set up at Grangemouth on the Forth, and Aberdeen and the east coast flourished as service centres and suppliers of platforms and equipment to a world-class industry.

North Sea oil and gas were of course British, not specifically Scottish, assets although nationalists disagreed. Nevertheless the benefits to local economies were obvious – so much so that, at the end of the 1990s, some pundits were predicting a gloomy future if existing fields became exhausted and new ones proved unviable; but nobody seemed to be certain whether or not this was likely to happen.

Meanwhile, other parts of Scotland adjusted to new realities. Electronics firms moved into Clydeside, which was dubbed 'Silicon Valley', and the growth of service industries, 'heritage' features and tourism made it apparent that Scotland had definitely entered the 'post-industrial' age.

MODERN AND POST-MODERN TIMES

SCOTLAND HAS COME TO TERMS WITH MODERNITY IN MANY WAYS. THE HIGHLANDS HAVE THEIR HYDROELECTRIC SCHEMES AND, MORE CONTROVERSIALLY, BRITAIN'S FIRST FAST-BREEDER NUCLEAR REACTOR, SITED ON THE NORTHERNMOST COAST AT DOUNREAY. THE TRIUMPH OF THE AUTOMOBILE HAS BEEN SIGNALLED BY, AMONG OTHER THINGS, ROAD BRIDGES ACROSS THE FORTH AND, TO THE DISMAY OF MANY, FROM THE MAINLAND TO THE ISLAND OF SKYE.

Modern and post-modern styles of architecture have become established in the form of housing estates, schools and universities, office buildings and shopping malls. New immigrants have enriched the ethnic diversity of the cities, although the urban population has nevertheless tended to shrink as the number of country-based car commuters rises.

Tourism is now one of Scotland's major industries, influencing the way in which many places, people and events present themselves to the world. There has been a reawakening to the value (monetary as well as spiritual) of the national culture, using the term in its widest sense to signify a way of life rather than an exclusive concentration on matters of art and intellect. In this area Edinburgh established a long lead, thanks to a handful of far-sighted individuals. In 1947 Rudolf Bing, manager of the Glyndebourne Opera Company, tried to interest a number of English cities in staging an international festival of music and drama. Preoccupied with bomb damage, reconstruction and austerity measures, they made no positive response; but when Bing approached Edinburgh, he found enthusiastic backers. The first Edinburgh Festival was held in August 1947 with Rudolf Bing as artistic director. It was also the first great post-war European festival, and as such attracted famous musicians and orchestras, enjoyed an immediate success, and became a major annual event on the cultural calendar.

Once fairly launched, the Festival acted as a magnet that drew in other arts and entertainments. In 1950 the Edinburgh Military Tattoo was staged for the first time on the Castle Esplanade; featuring massed bands and precision displays of marching and drills, with a floodlit Edinburgh Castle in the background, the tattoo became one of the star

THE FINALE OF THE EDINBURGH MILITARY TATTOO, ONE OF THE MOST SPECTACULAR EVENTS IN THE ANNUAL EDINBURGH FESTIVAL. IT HAS BEEN STAGED SINCE 1950 ON THE ESPLANADE BESIDE THE CASTLE, BRIEFLY RESTORING IT TO ITS FORMER ROLE AS A PARADE GROUND, WITH THE ADDITION OF MARCHING BANDS AND IMMACULATELY-EXECUTED MILITARY FEATS.

attractions of the Festival. Even earlier additions were the shows put on by uninvited performers around the fringes of the Festival. Over the years these multiplied, and 'the Fringe' became a recognized institution, composed of individuals and groups from all over the world; by the 1990s they were occupying every available space in the city and putting on some five hundred performances a day during the Festival. Film, book and jazz festivals also became regular events, galleries large and small put on special exhibitions, buskers set up on the Royal Mile and at the bottom of the Mound, and for those with the requisite stamina the Festival weeks became a non-stop jamboree. The impulse given by the Festival helped to make Edinburgh more conscious of the role of the arts. Music had long been well catered for, but it was only in the 1960s that the capital acquired first-class theatre companies in the Traverse and the Royal Lyceum. By contrast, several companies were established in Glasgow during the 1930s and '40s, although only one, the Citizens' Theatre in the Gorbals, survived in the long term and established a more than local reputation. Glasgow's awakening took place amid the traumas of the 1980s, when the value of the city's Victorian heritage was realized and steps were taken to conserve it and, so far as was possible, make good the damage done in the past. Glasgow's heritage as an ancient university town was promoted, the Burrell Collection of works of art was housed in a splendid new museum, and Charles Rennie Mackintosh's buildings and designs became emblematic (perhaps to excess) of post-industrial Glasgow. In 1989 the transfer of the Scottish Youth Theatre from Edinburgh to Glasgow was seen by some as a straw in the wind, and after Glasgow became European City of Culture in 1990, the metropolis and the capital were competing on more or less equal terms for recognition as the guardians of the national heritage.

THE SKYE ROAD BRIDGE, LINKING THE KYLE OF LOCHALSH ON THE MAINLAND WITH KYLEAKIN. THE DECISION TO CONSTRUCT THE BRIDGE, WHICH WAS COMPLETED IN 1995, WAS THE SUBJECT OF MUCH CONTROVERSY, DESPITE THE STRAIN ON THE FERRIES IMPOSED BY A MILLION VISITORS INTENT ON GOING 'OVER THE SEA TO SKYE'.

A PARLIAMENT FOR THE PEOPLE

NEW M.P. WINIFRED EWING, NEWLY ELECTED SCOTTISH NATIONAL PARTY MEMBER FOR HAMILTON, ARRIVES WITH HER THREE CHILDREN TO TAKE HER SEAT IN THE HOUSE OF COMMONS. HER SENSATIONAL 1967 VICTORY WAS THE SNP'S FIRST SUBSTANTIAL SUCCESS IN THE THREE DECADES OF ITS EXISTENCE, HERALDING A PERIOD OF FLUCTUATING BUT GRADUALLY IMPROVING FORTUNES.

FOR MOST OF THE 20TH CENTURY, SCOTTISH POLITICIANS ADHERED TO BRITISH PARTIES OF THE RIGHT, LEFT OR CENTRE AND HOPED TO CARRY OUT THEIR PROGRAMMES THROUGH THE PARLIAMENT AT WESTMINSTER. KEIR HARDIE, JAMES MAXTON AND RAMSAY MACDONALD SOUGHT TO ACHIEVE RADICAL OR SOCIALIST GOALS; BALFOUR, DOUGLAS-HOME AND IAIN MACLEOD REPRESENTED DIFFERENT SHADES OF CONSERVATISM.

The way in which Scots cast their votes suggested that their political outlook was also British and international; insofar as their grievances and resentments were directed against the British establishment, they took the form of voting Liberal or Labour (one or the other held a majority of Scottish seats for almost the entire 20th century) or giving a degree of support to far-left groupings such as the Independent Labour and Communist Parties. Some measure of Scottish self-government or 'Home Rule' was at times viewed sympathetically by British governments, but the issue never seemed urgent, and as the Labour Party became the dominant political force in Scotland, most Scots pinned their hopes on policies (nationalization, welfare measures, subsidies) to be implemented by a strong central government at Westminster.

There were always some Scots who felt differently and hankered after Home Rule or even independence. The National Party of Scotland was founded in 1928, merging with the Scottish Party in 1934 to form the Scottish National Party (SNP). Apart from isolated successes (victory in a protest by-election, the election of the popular novelist Compton Mackenzie as rector of Glasgow) the SNP made little impression until 1967, when Winnie Ewing was unexpectedly elected at Hamilton. After this the SNP's fortunes fluctuated wildly, but there seemed to be a long-term tendency for its support to increase. By this time the SNP was committed to outright independence for Scotland, and the finds of North Sea oil and gas in the 1970s made it easier for the party to argue that the country would not suffer any economic loss if the Union was dissolved. Though the Nationalists were far from securing a majority of Scottish votes, they were enough of a threat to convince the main parties that it would be prudent to concede some degree of self-government, which was now described as devolution. Yet in 1979, when a Labour government put a devolution scheme to the Scottish electorate, the outcome was a fiasco. The narrowest possible majority voted in favour, the turnout was low, and the Yes vote failed to secure the support of 40 per cent of the electorate, which had been stipulated as the minimum required if devolution was to go ahead. (Critics saw the stipulation as an undemocratic barrier raised by covert Unionists; others argued that it was reasonable to implement a major constitutional change only if it could be shown to command substantial support.) At the subsequent general election, the collapse of the SNP vote seemed to confirm that Scots, like other British people, cared more about economic issues than constitutional matters or even nationhood. Signs of a change of heart appeared soon afterwards. The general election of 1979 brought to power a Conservative Party whose policies were deeply unpopular in Scotland but brought it victory south of the border and consequently parliamentary majorities. Since this situation lasted for seventeen years, the disadvantages of being governed in all things from Westminster became glaringly obvious when Scots voted overwhelmingly against a set of policies but were subjected to them all the same. By the 1970s polls were showing high levels of support for devolution or even independence; these were only partly translated into votes for a revived SNP, since the dominant Scottish party, Labour, had again become committed to devolution. After a landslide victory in the 1997 general election, a new Labour government submitted devolution proposals which received a much more convincing endorsement than those of 1979. The devolved Scottish parliament was to remain subject to the sovereignty of Westminster, but would take control of health, education, law and order, local government and similar subjects, receiving a block grant and exercising limited powers to vary United Kingdom rates of taxation. The intention was to satisfy the Scots' wish for self-government; pessimists feared, and nationalists hoped, that devolution would prove to be a first step towards the break-up of the Union. After the first purely Scottish parliamentary elections, Labour remained easily the largest party, forming a coalition government with the Liberal Democrats; the SNP became the official opposition. Whatever the future might hold, most Scots were proud and pleased when, in May 1999, members of the new Parliament in Edinburgh were sworn in, and what had been described in 1707 as 'the end of an auld song' proved to be merely a lengthy interruption.

NEW PARLIAMENT. AFTER THE 1997 SCOTTISH REFERENDUM, WORK BEGAN ON A NEW PARLIAMENT BUILDING AT THE FOOT OF CALTON HILL, EDINBURGH: THE MODEL (BELOW) ENTHUSED POLITICIANS AND ARCHITECTS, IF NOT THE GENERAL PUBLIC. MEANWHILE IN 1999 THE ELECTED PARLIAMENTARIANS MET IN THE CHURCH OF SCOTLAND ASSEMBLY HALL CLOSE TO THE ROYAL MILE.

INDEX

ACKNOWLEDGMENTS

Niall Benvie 8 **Bodleian Library** (Ms Arch.Seld.B24 f.192r) 96 **Bridgeman Art Library,** London/New York 107 top, 146/British Library 24, 29, 32 top/City of Edinburgh Museums & Art Galleries 47, 72 bottom, 92-93/City Museum & Art Gallery, Stoke-on-Trent © Eduardo Paolozzi 2000 All Rights Reserved, DACS 123/Fine Art Society, London 121 top, 140/Robert Fleming Holdings Ltd, London 41, 121 bottom/Giraudon/Musée Ingres, Montauban 101 top/Guildhall Art Gallery,Corporation of London 114-115/Guildhall Library, Corporation of London 56/Heeresgeschichtliches Museum, Vienna 65 top/Houses of Parliament, Westminster, London 39/Lincolnshire County Council, Usher Gallery, Lincoln 31/National Gallery of Scotland 42, 51, 75 top, 78 right, 118, 119/National Gallery of Victoria, Melbourne, Australia 120/National Museum of Antiquities, Edinburgh 19 left/O'Shea Gallery, London 70/Private Collections 38, 64, 65 bottom, 87, 112 top/Royal Holloway & Bedford New College, Surrey 48/Science Museum, London 62-63/Scottish National Gallery of Modern Art, Edinburgh 122/Scottish National Portrait Gallery 26, 28, 36, 37 top, 40, 54, 60-61, 66, 99, 100, 102, 104, 106/Stapleton Collection 85/Victoria & Albert Museum 30, 79, 117/John Hay Whitney Collection, New York 93, 108/Wingfield Sporting Gallery, London 89 top/Yale Center for British Art, Paul Mellon Collection 8-9 **City of Edinburgh Museums**/Huntly House Museum 32 bottom/The People's Story Museum 46 **Colorsport** 91 **E.T. Archive** 25 **Mary Evans Picture Library** 80, 110 **Historic Scotland**/© crown copyright reserved 23, 27 **Doug Houghton** 4, 16 bottom, 94, 131 **Hulton Getty Picture Collection** 26-27, 28-29, 33, 34 left, 42-43, 44, 45, 57, 59 top, 59 bottom, 60, 63 top, 63 bottom, 69, 71 right, 74, 75 bottom, 77 bottom, 86, 90, 92, 95, 98 bottom, 98-99, 103 top, 103 bottom, 105, 108-109, 109, 125, 126, 137, 143, 154 **A.F. Kersting** 35, 40-41, 133 bottom, 134, 138, 139 **Kobal Collection**/BBC Scotland/Ecosse Films 126-127/Walt Disney 55/Figment/Noel Gay/Channel 4 113 bottom/Gaumont-British 112 bottom **Mander & Mitchenson** 113 top **Museum of Scotland** 34 right, 148 top **National Library of Scotland, Manuscript Division** 124/Roxburghe Estates 21 **National Library of Scotland, Rare Books Division** 98 top **National Monuments Record of Scotland** 76 **The Trustees of the National Museums of Scotland 2000** 84 **National Trust for Scotland Photo Library** 16-17, 128, 128-129, 135, 141/Val Bissland 50/Douglas MacGregor 147/Glyn Satterley 14/Harvey Wood 68-69, 136 **Octopus Publishing Group Ltd** 58, 67, 77 top, 83, 101 bottom, 107 bottom, 111/National Museums of Scotland 114 left/Scottish United Services Museum 84-85 **Public Record Office** 22 **Scotland in Focus** front cover top, front cover bottom, 10, 46-47, 71 left, 130-131/A. Barnes 7, 153 bottom/D. Barnes back cover, 9/J. Byers 12/L. Campbell 3, 10-11,13 132/B. Chapple 19 right, 152/G. Corbett 150-151/A. Cringean 153 top/P. Davies 82/R.G. Elliott 144-145, 148-149/J. Guidi 16 top, 78 left/D.Houghton 18/A.G. Johnston 144, 151/B. Lawson 20, 53/J. MacPherson 89 bottom/P. McGrath 148 bottom/I. McLean 146-147/S. McMillan 72-73/M. Moar 81, 132, 140-141, 142, 145, 150/C.K. Robeson 52/R. Schofield back cover flap, 133 top, 136-137/J. Weir 130/R. Weir 14-15, 129/Willbir 88, 114 right/G. Williams 116 **Scottish Parliament** 155 **Still Moving Picture Company**/Anne Burgess 124-125/©STB 72 top, 97 **V & A Picture Library,** 49